FROM A BROOM CUPBOARD

From a broom cupboard

20 YEARS OF RURAL HEALTH AT MONASH

Edited by Robert Clough

© Copyright 2012
Copyright of the individual works belongs to the individual authors.
Copyright of this collection as a whole belongs to Robert Clough.

All rights reserved. Apart from any uses permitted by Australia's Copyright Act 1968, no part of this book may be reproduced by any process without prior written permission from the copyright owners. Inquiries should be directed to the publisher.

Published by Monash University Publishing on behalf of
The School of Rural Health, Monash University.

Monash University Publishing
Building 4, Monash University
Clayton, Victoria 3800, Australia
www.publishing.monash.edu

Monash University Publishing brings to the world publications which advance the best traditions of humane and enlightened thought.

ISBN: 978-1-921867-98-9

www.publishing.monash.edu/books/fbc-9781921867989.html

Cover design: Steve Kirkbright
Cover images: Steve Kirkbright

Printed in Australia by Griffin Press an Accredited ISO AS/NZS 14001:2004 Environmental Management System printer.

The paper this book is printed on is certified by the Programme for the Endorsement of Forest Certification scheme. Griffin Press holds PEFC chain of custody SGS - PEFC/COC-0594. PEFC promotes environmentally responsible, socially beneficial and economically viable management of the world's forests.

FOREWORD

As Vice Chancellor of Monash University, I congratulate the School of Rural Health on a stunning 20 years of growth and commitment to improving rural health.

My first interaction with the Monash University Centre for Rural Health was through its Primary Care Clinic in Bendigo. I was a visiting neurologist and practised from a room at the clinic once a week. I was impressed that the clinic provided much needed bulk-billed primary care services to a relatively large proportion of the local population who, because of the shortage of general practitioners, could not get in to see a regular general practitioner or could not afford to pay the gap payment. An added benefit was the relief the service provided to the hospital emergency department by dealing with many of the sub-acute presentations that overwhelmed that service. It was rare to see a university department so involved with grass roots health care and community service.

In 2003 I became the dean of the Faculty of Medicine, Nursing and Health Sciences at Monash University and again was able to appreciate the work of the School of Rural Health, albeit from a completely different perspective. I was most impressed with work that the school was performing. The undergraduate clinical medical training in rural locations was first-class, lauded by the students and reflected in their results. The research produced by the school was thorough, pertinent and insightful. On top of its excellent academic programs the school was well managed and administered, a situation of some consequence to the incoming dean! Again it was obvious that the School of Rural Health had embedded itself within the communities from which it operated, playing an integral role within the health care environment. These views were reinforced whenever I spoke to bureaucrats, community leaders or health service providers. The School of Rural Health was one of the jewels in the crown of the Faculty of Medicine, Nursing and Health Sciences at Monash University.

More recently I have observed and been impressed with the growth of the school from my position of Vice-Chancellor at Monash University.

In the pages that follow you will read contributions from many authors that, when read together, provide a rich tapestry that tells the story of the school's evolution. This is a history of a unit that has always been ahead of the game. Whether in rural medical education, research into rural health or advocacy for rural health issues, this school has consistently provided the ideas, applications and reviews that have resulted in templates for others to follow. These examples have been observed and applied both nationally and internationally.

The book includes a fascinating insight from the Centre for Rural Health's founder, Professor Roger Strasser, into the ideas and events that culminated in the centre's establishment. Roger writes of the underlying concepts and the activities the centre undertook in the 1990s. Many of the co-authors remark on his relentless passion for rural health issues and this is still remarkably evident in his writing in the first chapter.

Professor John Humphreys's chapter on the history of research at the school is comprehensive and reflective of not only the unit's output, but of the output of the entire sector over this time.

Professor Geoff Solarsh became head of school in 2004. Geoff led the school into another era as the regional clinical schools consolidated and an increasing number of undergraduate medical students received their clinical training under their care. Geoff's important chapter details the changes during this time and events that culminated in the establishment of the Northern Victoria Regional Medical Education Network and the groundbreaking partnership with the University of Melbourne.

At the beginning of 2011 another important milestone was achieved when, under Professor Judi Walker's leadership, the Gippsland Medical School was amalgamated with the School of Rural Health. As originally conceived and established, Gippsland Medical School was in an ambivalent position in relation to the regional clinical schools in Gippsland and this move relieved the tensions generated by different approaches to rural medical education and competition for clinical places in Gippsland, paving the way for the next era in the School of Rural Health's growth and development.

The thoughtful and considered contributions from people both internal and external to the School of Rural Health provide views from different perspectives and, together, a comprehensive narrative of the evolution of the school.

While celebrating what has been achieved and learning the lessons of history, current head of school, Professor Judi Walker, has written a final chapter that looks forward to an exciting future with a bubbling passion reminiscent of that displayed 20 years earlier.

Roger Strasser, John Humphreys and Judi Walker were part of the original group of like-minded clinicians and academics often referred to in Australia as the 'rural health mafia' due to their single-minded dedication to the cause. Monash University is proud of the School of Rural Health. This publication is an exceptional record, explaining how the school has evolved, and a worthy celebration of what has been achieved.

Professor Ed Byrne, AO
Vice-Chancellor and President
Monash University

CONTENTS

Foreword v
Contributors x
Acknowledgements xvii
Acronyms xviii
Preface xix

1. The early years: Initial vision and foundation 1
   Professor Roger Strasser

2. Changing emphasis: Monash University
   Department of Rural and Indigenous Health 17
   *Professor Elaine Duffy, Professor Peter O'Meara, Dr Janice Chesters,
   Dr Jo Wainer, AM, Mollie Burley*

3. External environment: The view from the outside 35
   *The Hon. Dr Michael Wooldridge, Robert Wells, Di Wyatt,
   Emeritus Professor Nicholas Saunders, AO, Dane Huxley*

4. Rural medical training: Applying the curriculum
   in a rural environment 49
   *Dr John Togno, Associate Professor David Campbell, Professor
   Gordon Whyte, Dr Ryan Spencer, John Clark, Elyssia Bourke*

5. Collaboration in northern Victoria: Embedding education
   in regional health services and communities 72
   Professor Geoff Solarsh

6. Research: Community relevance 90
   Emeritus Professor John S Humphreys

7. Aboriginal health: Leading the way 112
   Associate Professor Marlene Drysdale

8. Administration: Flying under the radar 121
   Robert Clough

9. Gippsland Medical School: Taking advantage
   of opportunities as they arise 136
   *Associate Professor William Hart, Professor Judi Walker, Associate
   Professor Shane Bullock*

Afterword: Learning from the past for a sustainable future 146
Professor Judi Walker

CONTRIBUTORS

Elyssia Bourke

Originally from Cardigan near Ballarat, Elyssia is a medical student currently on intermission as she completes a Bachelor of Medical Science degree. She is an Extended Rural Cohort student committed to spending five-sixths of her three clinical training years in rural areas. Her Year 3 was spent in Mildura then in Year 4 she spent one semester of rural GP training in Gisborne and one with specialist-based practices in regional Bendigo. Elyssia has held significant positions within Wildfire, including terms as secretary and co-president.

Mollie Burley

Apart from a four-year break, Mollie has been continuously involved with rural health at Monash since its inception. Mollie has worked on numerous education programs and research projects. Along the way she has developed expertise and passion for enhancing collaboration between health professions, with the aim of bridging the theory and service divide. Mollie currently leads the interprofessional collaboration team within the Monash University Department of Rural and Indigenous Health, and the Placement, Education and Research Unit at Latrobe Community Health Services.

Associate Professor David Campbell

After many years of involvement with GP training, David was first appointed as a 0.1 fractional-time senior lecturer in 1999. He later became the inaugural director of the East Gippsland Regional Clinical School, a position he still holds today. David is passionate about the virtues of rural clinical practice in the provision of health care as well as in undergraduate and postgraduate training. He has served many leadership roles outside Monash – the most recent being as president of the Australian College of Rural and Remote Medicine – and has played a leading role on key committees and with the Rural Workforce Agency of Victoria. Along with leading the East Gippsland Regional Clinical School, David continues to practise as a GP in Lakes Entrance.

Dr Janice Chesters

Janice worked with rural health at Monash between 1999 and 2010, commencing as a lecturer and advancing to associate professor and acting director of the Monash University Department of Rural and Indigenous Health. During this time Janice worked on a wide variety of projects including the Master of Rural Health, developing rural aspects of the new five-year medical curriculum, the Building Healthy Communities Project and the Footprints Forwards Project that presented strategies for improving recruitment, retention and support of Aboriginal medical students. Janice is currently the director of Awhina, the Waitemata Health Campus, and an adjunct professor at AUT University Auckland, New Zealand. She pursues a conviction that the future of health care and health care education lies in close collaboration between health care providers, universities and other training providers.

John Clark

John hails from Donald, a community of 1700 people in Victoria's north-west. After completing year 12 at Donald High School, he moved to Clayton to undertake the first two years of the medical program. He has spent a further two years completing clinical training in Mildura, Bendigo and Kyneton. John is currently studying for a Bachelor of Medical Science; he is working on a research project at the Royal Children's Hospital Melbourne, but continues to maintain a rural interest as a National Rural Health Students' Network medical representative and co-president of Wildfire. He will complete the final year of his undergraduate medical training in 2013, rotating through hospitals in Melbourne, London, Mildura and Bendigo.

Robert Clough

Rob was the manager of the Centre for Rural Health and the School of Rural Health from December 1998 to December 2010. During that time the organisation expanded from one primary site in Gippsland to eight major locations and 30 teaching general practices along a broad diagonal geographical slash: across Victoria from Mildura, through to East Gippsland. In that time staff numbers rose from 45 to over 320, while the expenditure budget expanded from around $2 million to over $30 million. Since leaving Monash, Rob has spent his time writing short stories and playing lawn bowls.

Adjunct Professor Marlene Drysdale

Recruited to establish and lead the Indigenous Health Unit in 2003, Marlene remained in this role until 2011. Under her direction the unit established and taught Aboriginal health subjects in all Monash's Faculty of Medicine, Nursing and Health Sciences courses. The unit also performed important research, and advocated and facilitated improved pathways for Aboriginal students into health courses. Marlene is currently employed as the senior Aboriginal health training advisor for the General Practitioner Education and Training Program in Canberra.

Professor Elaine Duffy

Commencing in 1995 on a 12-month secondment, Elaine remained until 2003. She advocated strongly for a balanced emphasis in the organisation's activities for nursing and the other non-medical health professions. Elaine held the position of deputy head for most of her tenure with rural health at Monash and became acting head on Roger's departure. Elaine was the inaugural head of the Centre for Multi-Disciplinary Studies in Rural Health. She is currently head of the School of Nursing and Midwifery at Griffith University in Queensland.

Emeritus Professor John S Humphreys

A geographer by training, John was Professor of Rural Health Research and head of the research unit at the School of Rural Health from 2002 until his retirement in 2012. During this time the organisation's research output and reputation for academic rigour increased substantially. John has been recognised over the years through a number of awards, the most recent being an honorary fellowship of the Australian College of Rural and Remote Medicine in 2010. These days John continues to be actively involved in research, as a chief investigator with the Centre for Research Excellence in Rural and Remote Primary Health Care, and in a number of his own projects. Any spare time created by his retirement is devoted to his family and pursuing his hobby of bird watching.

Dane Huxley

As the chief executive officer of the Mildura Base Hospital, Dane was approached to support the establishment of a clinical school in collaboration with his hospital. This began a long and fruitful relationship between Monash and Mildura Base Hospital that has seen the development of the clinical school and a number of multidisciplinary educational and research programs. Dane remains in his role with the hospital and is able to reflect on the advances that have been made.

Steve Kirkbright

Steve was with rural health at Monash from 1998 till 2006. He worked at various times as a project officer, lecturer, researcher and manager of multimedia and communications. His high quality graphic design skills created a 'look' that was instantly recognised and envied by those who encountered it through publications, posters, presentations and websites. He is currently working as a curriculum specialist at ERGT Australia, a safety training organisation.

Professor Peter O'Meara

Peter's first involvement with the Centre for Rural Health was in the mid-1990s in his role as general manager of the Gippsland ambulance service when the two organisations worked together to integrate the role of ambulance service medical officer into the centre's education program. He took up part-time employment with the centre in 1997 as a research assistant before later filling the role of full-time resources manager. Peter eventually moved to a full-time academic role, teaching within medical, nursing and rural health programs, as well as undertaking research. He completed his PhD examining rural ambulance services in Victoria during this time. Peter is currently the inaugural chair of Rural and Regional Paramedicine at La Trobe University in Bendigo.

Emeritus Professor Nicholas Saunders, AO

Nick was dean of the Faculty of Medicine, Nursing and Health Sciences from 1998 until 2002. This was a time of significant internal faculty change that included an organisational restructure and the introduction of a five-year medical curriculum. This period coincided with remarkable advances for rural health at Monash with recognition in the form of school status within the faculty and huge growth following the successful application for Commonwealth Rural Clinical School Project funding. Nick provided exceptional support and guidance for rural health during his time at Monash and even acted as head of school for a short period. In 2002 Nick was awarded the Centenary Medal from the Australian Government for his contribution to academic medicine. In 2012 he was appointed an Officer of the Order of Australia for distinguished service to medicine and higher education, and for his significant contribution to national academic and professional organisations.

Professor Geoff Solarsh

Geoff was recruited from South Africa as head of school in 2004 and remained in that position until 2007. This was a period of consolidation and refinement of medical education at Monash and the roles that the regional clinical schools performed. Geoff was also the regional director of the Bendigo Regional Clinical School and was pivotal in establishing the Northern Victoria Regional Medical Education Network – a collaboration with the University of Melbourne. Subsequently, Geoff stepped aside as head of school to concentrate on his role as head of the Monash University responsibilities within the network. Geoff continues in this capacity and as a paediatrician in Bendigo.

Dr Ryan Spencer

Ryan studied undergraduate medicine at Monash from 2002 until 2006. He grew up in Riddells Creek, on the train line to Bendigo, and became involved with Wildfire – the Monash University rural health club – while studying medicine. Through his role as the president of Wildfire he was involved in the roll-out of the new curriculum's significant rural component. He spent two years of his undergraduate training in Bendigo and East Gippsland. Ryan is an advanced trainee in cardiology and recently returned to Bendigo as a cardiology registrar on rotation from Austin Health.

Professor Roger Strasser, AM

Roger was the founder and spiritual leader of rural health at Monash for the first 10 years, and it was primarily his vision, opportunism and enthusiasm that drove the organisation during that era. He was the first Professor of Rural Health and led the first academic unit of its type: the Centre for Rural Health. Roger left Monash in 2002 to become the founding dean of the Northern Ontario School of Medicine, a position he still holds. In 2011, he was appointed a Member of the Order of Australia for his service to medicine. As an educator, researcher and practitioner Roger has improved health care for people living in rural and remote communities in both developed and developing nations.

Dr John Togno

A strong advocate of the virtues of immersion in rural practice in undergraduate medical training, John was an early recruit to the Centre for Rural Health. He had established the Primary Care Clinic in Bendigo within the Monash Department of Community Medicine, but his vision was more closely aligned with the Centre for Rural Health following its establishment. The clinic became part of the Centre for Rural Health a short time later. John was the leader of the medical education stream during the development of the five-year medical curriculum and played a significant role in infusing a strong rural flavour into it. John is currently a GP in Bendigo and a medical educator in an Australian College of Rural and Remote Medicine pilot program.

Adjunct Associate Professor Jo Wainer, AM

Jo was involved directly with rural health at Monash from 1997 until 2010. Jo's interest in gender and medicine was expressed through her research as well as curriculum development and teaching. She also played central roles for the organisation in strategic development, research leadership and executive committee involvement at various times. In 2010 Jo was appointed a Member of the Order of Australia for service to the community as an academic and researcher of women's reproductive health rights, and through leadership roles promoting women in medicine, particularly in rural and remote areas.

Professor Judi Walker

Judi became head of the School of Rural Health at Monash in November 2010. Her credentials include vast experience in the development of academic rural health in Australia. She has witnessed the development of rural health at Monash and had working relationships with many of its members, long before her commencement. Judi's knowledge of the school's past and its people, coupled with an understanding of the environment in which it operates, ideally places her to lead it towards an exciting future.

Robert Wells

Robert Wells is a former first assistant secretary in the Commonwealth Department of Health and Ageing where he was involved in research policy, Commonwealth/state relations, health workforce, rural health programs, safety and quality as well as programs for better management of mental health and major diseases such as cancer and diabetes. He managed the

Commonwealth's health workforce programs from the early 1990s and left the department in 2004. Currently Robert is the director of the Australian Primary Health Care Research Institute and the Menzies Centre for Health Policy at the Australian National University.

Adjunct Professor Gordon Whyte

After 12 years as head of the Red Cross Blood Bank, Gordon's desire to try something different led to his appointment as the first director of the Bendigo Regional Clinical School in 2001. Gordon's understanding of systems engineering proved invaluable, not only in establishing the clinical school in Bendigo but later for the faculty, in installing their medical course in Sharjah, one of the United Arab Emirates, and then in curriculum design and implementation at Monash. Gordon had a short stint as head of school in 2003 then came back as head of school from the beginning of 2008 until late 2010. Gordon recently retired from paid academic service but continues to feed his thirst for knowledge through Master of Arts research into the history of clinical reasoning.

The Hon. Dr Michael Wooldridge

Michael was the federal Minister for Health from 1995 until 2001. During his time in office many innovative rural health initiatives were introduced including the John Flynn Scholarship Scheme, the University Departments of Rural Health Program and the Rural Clinical Schools Program. These programs had a profound effect, not least on the evolution of rural health at Monash. Michael is currently an adjunct professorial fellow at Monash University and chairs two cooperative research centres at the University of Melbourne.

Di Wyatt

Di was the manager of the Victorian Department of Human Services' rural health unit during the early and mid-1990s. She became the executive director of the Victorian Universities Rural Health Consortium later that decade, worked with the Monash School of Rural Health as director of business and development, and then in international development in the early 2000s. Di currently works for the Australian College of Rural and Remote Medicine as strategic projects manager.

ACKNOWLEDGEMENTS

A book such as this is always the work of many people. 'Thank you' to the authors who have donated their time and expertise to write their view of the evolution of rural health at Monash. Together, their stories provide a multi-perspective view of this history.

There were others who also made significant contributions. Steve Kirkbright designed the cover and contributed many of the images found in this book. Ann Dettrick brought her editorial skills, enthusiasm and positive support to the project, Melissa McNicol was generous with editorial advice and Gillian Fallon was meticulous in her proof reading. Helen Cronin's attention to detail, drive and expertise were the backbone of this project; without her this book would have remained at the good idea stage.

Like a book, an organisation such as the School of Rural Health is always the work of many people. The combined energy and dedication of hundreds of former and present staff members have made the School of Rural Health what it is today. There are too many to mention individually; however, their efforts are appreciated. They should be proud of what they have achieved.

ACRONYMS

ACRRM	Australian College of Rural and Remote Medicine
CMDS	Centre for Multi-Disciplinary Studies in Rural Health
GAMSAT	Graduate Medical School Admissions Test
GOODies	Group for Organisational Overview and Development
GPET	General Practice Education and Training
MBBS	Bachelor of Medicine/Bachelor of Surgery – undergraduate medical degree
MUDRIH	Monash University Department of Rural and Indigenous Health
MURPA	Monash Undergraduate Research Projects Abroad
NHMRC	National Health and Medical Research Council
NVRMEN	Northern Victoria Regional Medical Education Network
OSCE	Objective structured clinical examination
RCS	Rural clinical school, or regional clinical school
SPECTRUM	Support Program for Education and Clinical Training of Rural Undergraduates in Mildura
UDRH	University department of rural health
UMAT	Undergraduate Medicine and Health Sciences Admission Test
VTAC	Victorian Tertiary Admissions Centre
Wonca	Short name for World Organization of National Colleges, Academies and Academic Associations of General Practitioners/Family Physicians.

PREFACE

It is 20 years since the establishment of the Monash University Centre for Rural Health in 1992. Those 20 years have seen Australia's first rural academic unit, located in a former broom cupboard at the Latrobe Valley Hospital in Moe, evolve into a multi-site school with significant facilities in Mildura, Bendigo, Moe, Traralgon, Sale and Bairnsdale, and many smaller facilities dotted elsewhere across Victoria. During this evolution it has been at the forefront of rural health teaching, research, development, advocacy and practice locally, nationally and internationally. Many dedicated people have played significant roles, and many events have altered the course of the organisation's development and influence.

This book is a celebration of Monash University School of Rural Health's twentieth anniversary. The aim of the publication is to tell the story of the school's evolution using the unique perspectives of a number of authors. These authors – from inside and outside the organisation – have written, from their respective vantage points, of what they saw and experienced of the school's maturation. When read together their contributions provide a rich collage of the school's history.

Roger Strasser explains the chain of ideas and events that led to the 'cleaners' store' at the Moe Hospital. He expands on the ever-increasing surge of projects and programs as the organisation's activities and influence grew over the first 10 years. Elaine Duffy, Janice Chesters and others contribute to a chapter focusing on the non-medical training streams of activity that have ultimately come together as the Monash University Department of Rural and Indigenous Health (MUDRIH). This chapter also explains the changing emphases and influences throughout the organisation's history. An external view of the organisation is provided in chapter three where relationships with public service organisations, the faculty and health services are reviewed. This chapter also includes an account by Michael Wooldridge of the political environment that lead to the introduction of the University Departments of Rural Health and Rural Clinical Schools programs.

Undergraduate medical training was the original activity of the newly formed Centre for Rural Health and has continued for two decades. However, from the introduction of the regional clinical schools, the number of students – undergraduate and graduate entry – receiving their training within the School of Rural Health has grown immensely. The number of medical students placed within the school in 2012 is 703 while there have been 7,549 placements since 2003. John Togno, David Campbell and Gordon Whyte elaborate on how this was achieved, while former medical student Ryan Spencer and current students Elyssia Bourke and John Clark give their perspectives of the clinical training they received. Geoff Solarsh's chapter explains the establishment of the Northern Victoria Regional Medical Education Network, in collaboration with the University of Melbourne, and the innovative medical training programs they run.

John Humphreys's chapter, which reviews research activity, is as rigorous and thorough as could be expected from Australia's pre-eminent rural health researcher. He details the consistent and methodical growth in research output and elaborates on many of the highlights of the past 20 years.

Another important stream of activity for rural health at Monash has been Aboriginal and Torres Strait Islander health. Marlene Drysdale established the Indigenous Health Unit in 2002 and led it until 2011. During that period the unit had remarkable successes which included providing cultural training for staff and students across the faculty, completing major research projects and introducing a process for enhanced recruitment and support for Aboriginal students. Marlene writes of these developments and the recognition and use of the unit's principles to establish the School of Indigenous Health.

I have written about the school's development from an administrative perspective. In a short period of time the organisation grew from a small department, unnoticed by central administration, to a $30 million school that made the headlines.

Judi Walker's feet have barely touched the ground since her appointment as head of school in late 2010. Judi writes of the merger of the Gippsland Medical School with the School of Rural Health and how this has been achieved. In the final chapter Judi looks back on the history and how it is reflected in the current School of Rural Health and what promises it holds for the future.

The 20 years from 1992 have seen a wave of changes in rural health, commencing as recognition of the issues and building in strength and momentum as solutions have been formulated and implemented. Rural health at Monash University has been surfing this wave from the beginning and the following pages relive that ride.

Robert Clough

The first 20 years of the School of Rural Health

Year	Event
1992	Centre for Rural Health established
1993	Bendigo division established
	Bendigo Primary Care Clinic transferred from Monash Community Medicine to Centre for Rural Health
1998	Move from Moe to Traralgon
2000	Position of Professor of Rural Health Research established
2001	School of Rural Health established
	Rural clinical school funding approved
	Mildura Regional Clinical School established
	Bendigo Regional Clinical School established
	Gippsland Regional Clinical School established
	East Gippsland Regional Clinical School established
2002	Centre for Multi-Disciplinary Studies in Rural Health established
	Roger Strasser departed for Canada
	Elaine Duffy acting head of school
2003	Elaine Duffy departed for Canada
	John Humphreys, Gordon Whyte acting heads of school
2004	Nick Saunders acting head of school
	Geoff Solarsh commenced as head of school
2006	Northern Victoria Regional Medical Education Network (NVRMEN) established
	Monash University Department of Rural and Indigenous Health (MUDRIH) superseded the Centre for Multi-Disciplinary Studies in Rural Health
	Gippsland Medical School established
2008	Gordon Whyte head of school
2010	Judi Walker commenced as head of school
2011	Centre for Research Excellence in Rural and Remote Primary Health Care established
	Gippsland Medical School and School of Rural Health amalgamated
2012	Twentieth anniversary of School of Rural Health

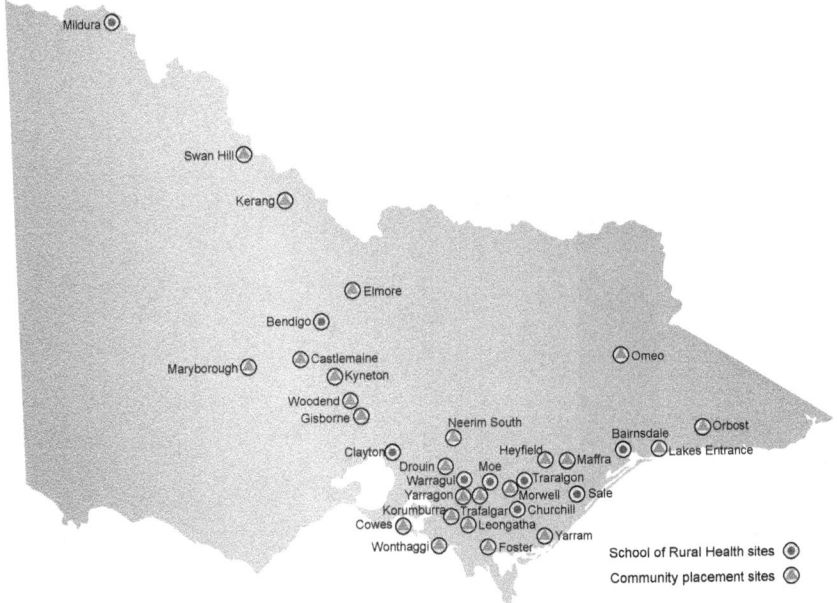

The School of Rural Health's footprint in 2012.

CHAPTER 1

THE EARLY YEARS: INITIAL VISION AND FOUNDATION

PROFESSOR ROGER STRASSER

After graduating from Monash in 1977, I completed an internship at Prince Henry's Hospital and then undertook general practice training before travelling to the United Kingdom where I met and married Sarah. We then moved to Canada where I undertook academic training at the University of Western Ontario and Sarah completed her general practice training. For me, the evolution of the School of Rural Health at Monash University began in late 1985 when Sarah and I moved to Gippsland from Canada and joined the Moe Medical Centre group practice.

In 1986, I took on the role of regional coordinator for the Royal Australian College of General Practitioners Family Medicine Program in Gippsland. Based on my experience in Britain and Canada, I encouraged the local hospitals and GPs to support the introduction of a Gippsland regional GP training program which would allow medical graduates to undertake all their GP training in the Gippsland region. To my disappointment, relatively small numbers of new graduates signed on for the regional program. This experience started me on the pathway which I am still following. I was very much enjoying life as a rural practitioner with many colleagues, but they were never sufficient in number. When I reviewed the literature and undertook research myself, I realised that the shortage of rural doctors was a problem that began in medical school or even before. Essentially, there were then very few medical students who came from rural areas, and rural practice was seen by the city-based senior medical school teachers as a career for those who could not succeed in other branches of medicine.

Through the late 1980s, rural doctors' associations in each Australian state were established and began pushing for new initiatives to overcome the chronic shortage of rural practitioners in all parts of Australia. In February 1991, the first National Rural Health Conference was held in Toowoomba, Queensland, and I was one of the invited participants. From this conference emerged Australia's first National Rural Health Strategy which included recommendations that all undergraduate professional education programs should require appropriate experience in a rural setting, and that regional hospitals should have a role in undergraduate education. To facilitate these recommendations, the strategy proposed the creation of academic departments in regional centres, which would also provide a better regional focus for continuing education, allowing rural practitioners a role in education, reducing professional isolation and creating a pool of locums.

Meanwhile in Gippsland in 1991, the process began of amalgamating the hospitals in Traralgon and Moe to form Latrobe Regional Health. The new hospital was to have a budget comparable with the Box Hill Hospital in Melbourne, and the Latrobe Regional Health leadership was attracted to the idea of hosting an academic unit. Seeing the opportunity, David Birks, a surgeon colleague at Moe Medical Centre, and I prepared a submission which was presented initially to Monash as part of a review of the Department of Medicine at the Alfred Hospital. David and I had worked together previously in 1989 to introduce a three-week rotation for Monash final year medical students to the hospital in Moe. This arrangement was supported by Paul O'Brien, then chair of surgery at the Alfred Hospital in Melbourne. In a sense, this three-week rotation was a sign of things to come. Prior to this, the only rural exposure Monash students had was four weeks in rural general practice, also in final year.

The dean of medicine at the time, Professor Bob Porter, was supportive of the proposal which was to establish a Monash University rural health academic unit at Latrobe Regional Health. This was different from the rural training units attached to regional hospitals of the time because of the university undergraduate medical education component. Other rural training units focused primarily on vocational training and continuing education. Neil Carson, chair of community medicine – later general practice – was overseas when the submission was presented, but he became an advocate within the faculty for the proposal after his return. It was interesting to watch as he persuaded other department chairs to support the proposal and then sought a financial contribution from them! The process was a bit like a poker game. Neil would say that he was putting in $50,000 and then challenged his colleague to 'see him' if not 'raise him'. During this process, I learnt that within the medical faculty 'multidiscipline' meant doctors in different medical specialties working together, whereas beyond the faculty, 'multidiscipline' referred to doctors, nurses and other health professionals working together.

Suffice it to say that the timing was right for this proposal which, with Neil Carson's sponsorship and Bob Porter's support, was ultimately approved by the faculty board. Prior to this formal approval, Bob Porter had encouraged me to apply for funding from the then new Commonwealth Rural Health Support Education and Training program.

The Centre for Rural Health was established in 1992 at the Moe campus of Latrobe Regional Health as Australia's first multidiscipline, multilevel rural health academic unit. I was fortunate to be appointed Australia's first Professor of Rural Health and director of the centre. The Centre for Rural Health began upstairs at Moe Hospital in a room which had been the cleaners' store. When Maria Harkom and I started, the cleaning materials had been removed but it took some time to organise furniture, telephones and office supplies.

Latrobe Regional Hospital, Moe, early 1990s: site of the original cleaners' store and now home of MUDRIH.

We developed a branch in Bendigo, based around the Primary Care Clinic which the Monash Department of Community Medicine had started in 1992. In 1998, the centre moved into purpose-built premises located at the new

Latrobe Regional Hospital on the highway west of Traralgon. Subsequently, the centre expanded to include Mildura in the network. In 2000, it was transformed into the Monash University School of Rural Health with the Centre for Multi-Disciplinary Studies in Rural Health based in Moe, and four regional clinical schools located in Mildura, Bendigo, Traralgon and Bairnsdale; each had a network of teaching and research sites distributed over the surrounding rural area.

We were successful in securing Commonwealth Government rural health funding and moved forward quickly with a range of education, research and community liaison initiatives networked across Gippsland and north-western Victoria. From the beginning, the focus was on working with people in rural and remote communities towards fulfilling the vision of improving rural health.

Educational initiatives included:

- rural clinical rotations and rural extracurricular activities for medical students
- interprofessional education initiatives
- collaboration with other Monash health programs including nursing, pharmacy, radiography and dietetics for rural clinical rotations
- promoting health careers to rural secondary students
- collaboration with the Royal Australian College of General Practitioners in developing rural GP training.

Subsequently, in 1998, the college and the Centre for Rural Health established the Gippsland Regional GP Training Program, 12 years after my initial attempt. In 1994, we introduced the Graduate Diploma and Master of Rural Health programs which offered graduate studies for rural health practitioners entirely by distance education. This program was redeveloped to be delivered online in 1998. In 1996, Amanda Young became the first of many rural health PhD students.

From the beginning, research was a major focus including studies of the rural health workforce, rural health services and specific health issues. Prior to 1991, research into the health of people living in rural and remote areas in Australia had been patchy and limited. In this context, the first National Rural Health Strategy recommended the establishment of a National Rural Health Unit which was subsequently funded by the Australian Health Ministers Advisory Council. We took the lead in a five-university

consortium which was successful in gaining funding in 1994 to establish what became known as the Australian Rural Health Research Institute. Institute activities included:
- redevelopment of the Rural Health Research Register which had been developed by the University of Queensland
- setting the agenda for collaborative rural health research
- projects on the use of communication information technology in rural and remote health
- a series of national rural health research workshops which brought together experienced researchers and novices.

In 2000, John Humphreys joined Monash as Australia's first Professor of Rural Health Research.

Collaborations and partnerships were a feature from the very beginning. These collaborations included:
- other Monash departments, centres and schools including those at Gippsland campus
- Latrobe Regional Health and other hospitals/health services throughout Gippsland and beyond
- divisions of general practice and related organisations
- vocational training organisations
- other universities and educational institutions
- government departments and agencies at local, state and federal levels.

Examples of successful collaborations included:
- the University of Melbourne, statewide coordination of rural GP placements and teacher training, followed later by the Victorian Advanced Training for General Practice program
- the Victorian Universities Rural Health Consortium involving five university partners
- Victorian Rural Divisions Coordinating Unit
- the Rural Workforce Agency Victoria
- the provision of ambulance medical officer services to Rural Ambulance Victoria in Gippsland.

During the early years of rapid growth and development there was also an increasing international dimension to the centre. Between 1992 and 2004, I was chair of the working party on rural practice of the World Organization of Family Doctors (Wonca) and we provided the secretariat. The Wonca working party on rural practice initiated a series of Wonca rural policy statements, rural health world conferences with associated conference declarations, and engagement with the World Health Organization. In 2002, as the School of Rural Health, we hosted the WHO–Wonca co-sponsored consultation – Health for All Rural People – which developed a global action plan for rural health. Also in 2002, in collaboration with other Australian organisations, we hosted the fifth Wonca World Rural Health Conference in Melbourne, which produced the 'Melbourne Manifesto: A Code of Practice for the International Recruitment of Health Care Professionals'.

In addition to the international networking through Wonca, we attracted many visitors from all parts of the world, including several individuals who undertook six-month sabbaticals. In 1994, Jim Rourke and his wife Lesley contributed to the early development of the centre and returned to Canada where Jim established the South Western Ontario Rural Medicine unit which was modelled on the Centre for Rural Health. Jim is now the dean of medicine at Memorial University of Newfoundland. Ian Couper came from South Africa in 1998 and has, since his return there, become Professor of Rural Health at Witwatersrand University in Johannesburg. In addition, Jim Rourke succeeded me as chair of the Wonca working party on rural practice, and Ian Couper succeeded Jim. The relationships which developed through these visits enriched the centre and enhanced Monash University's reputation as an international leader in academic rural health.

The people and the projects

There is no doubt that the rapid development and ongoing achievements of the Centre for Rural Health and later School of Rural Health are the direct result of the enthusiasm, commitment and hard work of the many, many people who have been part of it over the years. It was a great privilege and a real pleasure for me to be part of that talented and successful team during the first 10 years. There was a real sense of excitement as we were making it up as we went along, with associated wonderment when our efforts proved to be successful. I am not able to mention all the many people and projects but will highlight some which stand out in my mind.

Maria Harkom was the original administrative officer. She brought a positive, 'can do' approach which helped us all in those early years. Before long, Maria was joined by Elaine Evans who has continued with Monash to this day. Elaine's irrepressible cheerfulness and quirky sense of humour have helped us all through many ups and downs. As well as being my executive assistant, Elaine provided the secretariat for the Wonca working party on rural practice throughout my time as chair. In 1996, Elaine came with us to Shanghai for the first Wonca Rural Health World Conference and provided invaluable administrative support in a totally unfamiliar setting. I well remember her hilarious charade performance as she tried to explain to our Chinese hosts that we needed overhead projector sheets! Elaine's contribution was invaluable both to the success of that conference, which involved 300 rural practitioners from over 30 countries, and to the effectiveness of the Wonca working party on rural practice during its first 12 years. Over the years, Elaine's astute observations and commonsense approach have been a great strength.

David Birks is another stayer who has remained involved in one way or another from the beginning to this day. David's low-key manner can be deceptive. He is universally praised by medical students and other learners who have been fortunate to encounter him as a teacher in the classroom or in a clinical setting. Over the years, David has provided a cool and steady approach as a true psychological leader of the group. As well as teaching and leadership, David has undertaken research including the Special Cooperative Audit of Rural Surgery which gathered data demonstrating that the quality of rural surgical care is at least comparable with surgical care in metropolitan areas. David has also been active in many capacities with the Royal Australasian College of Surgeons over the years. For a time, he was in charge of the rural general surgery training stream for the college as well as participating on many college committees and in various education and outreach initiatives.

Although Associate Professor Elaine Duffy joined the Centre for Rural Health initially on secondment from the School of Nursing, she quickly became a key member of the team and stayed on in 1995 to become associate director/deputy head. Elaine brought her background in remote area nursing and a focus on multidisciplinary collaboration in rural health education, research and service to her new role. Her leadership ensured that the centre was recognised and respected beyond the world of medical education and medical practice, particularly among remote and rural nurses.

Another major contributor from the early days was Dr Robert Hall. I had known Robert since I was a medical student as he was one of the first national medical educators for the Family Medicine Program, which was later renamed the Royal Australian College of General Practitioners Training Program. For a time he was director of vocational training at Box Hill Hospital before moving to Gippsland as a goat farmer's husband. Over the years, Robert was involved in developing a range of new models of community health/general practice services, always with an emphasis on education and research. Robert provided significant leadership in education, particularly vocational training, and in research/development projects including the Rural Hospital Quality Assurance Project with the West Victoria Division of General Practice, the Extended Latrobe Valley Injury Study, the Rural Men's Health Project, and the Moe After Hours Medical Service. Robert was remarkable for his irrepressible creativity, boundless enthusiasm for innovation, and consistent tendency to think outside the box.

There were many general practitioners, particularly in Gippsland, who contributed to the development and implementation of rural health education and training. Dr Allin Marrow in Traralgon had worked with me as area coordinator when I was the Family Medicine Program regional coordinator and he continued to contribute through teaching medical students and vocational trainees. Dr David Campbell and Dr Patrick Kinsella in Lakes Entrance were also enthusiastic participants in rural GP training, and they contributed to the development of the Centre for Rural Health and later School of Rural Health. Dr Peter Stevens in Heyfield took on the role of program director of the Gippsland Regional GP Training Program. Among the other GP contributors over the years were Doctors Paul Flood, Sue Deed, Ken Mulligan, Darra Murphy, Brian Cole, James Brown, Chris Lampel, Charles Kerr, Gary Bourke, Leon Malzinzinskis and Sarah Strasser. Sarah had taken on leadership roles in rural GP vocational training nationally, but continued as a part-time senior lecturer at the Centre for Rural Health with particular responsibility for electives.

David Campbell undertook the Study of GPs in Towns Without Hospitals, as well as developing an increasing involvement in all aspects of rural medicine and rural medical education. This involvement included state and national leadership roles, including the presidency of the Australian College of Rural and Remote Medicine. When the East Gippsland Regional Clinical School was established, David became the director and continues in that role to this day.

Jane Greacen joined the Centre for Rural Health in 1997 after a period of working for the Victorian Government. She brought with her expertise in occupational health and public health which strengthened our education, research and workforce development activities. Subsequently, Jane was seconded to help establish the Rural Workforce Agency Victoria and stayed on as CEO.

Heather Kelly came to the centre with the idea for what became the A Great Career Where You Live Project which promoted health careers to rural secondary school students. This project – which included audiovisual materials and support for rural health professionals to present at local high schools – expanded to become a state-wide program with residential workshops in Melbourne. It also spawned similar programs in other states. Meanwhile, Heather became involved in various research and community projects including collaborative projects with the Centre for Research in Health, Education and Social Sciences at Monash Gippsland, led by David Harvey.

David Harvey and I were co-investigators on a series of studies focused on the health services in small rural communities, as well as a Study of Doctor and Patient Perceptions of General Practitioners as Resource Managers/Gatekeepers, and an evaluation of the Rural Health Support Education and Training Program.

Initially, Jo Wainer joined the Centre for Rural Health in 1995 as the research associate working on the Study of Health Service Delivery in Rural Communities. Subsequently, Jo, whose background is medical sociology, stayed with us as a senior lecturer involved in education and research. She focused particularly on her interest in gender in medicine, especially women in rural practice. This extended beyond Monash to the Australian College of Rural and Remote Medicine and internationally with the Wonca working party on rural practice. Jo went on to complete her PhD on women in medicine.

Bill Darmody, a partner in the Moe Veterinary Clinic, and his colleagues provided half-day case-based sessions for students to learn health issues at the human–animal interface. In addition, Bill organised for the students to visit local dairy farms and learn from the farmers about agricultural occupational health issues.

Anne Leversha combined her clinical pharmacy role at Latrobe Regional Hospital with a joint academic position that connected the Centre for Rural Health with the Victorian Pharmacy College, another faculty of Monash. Among Anne's contributions were: a teaching program on practical therapeutics for final year medical students; rural clinical placements for pharmacy students; and the Rural Pharmacist Support, Education and Training Project. Along the way, Anne attained a Master of Rural Health.

Dr John Togno was a driving force in initiating the Bendigo branch of the Centre for Rural Health. After establishing the Bendigo Primary Care Clinic, John became involved in a wide range of education and research activities. He took the lead in developing rural health options for medical students which were so popular that the faculty introduced a week-long rural medicine rotation for all Year 2 students. John's involvement in curriculum innovation came to the fore again through developing the rural health curriculum for the new five-year medicine course introduced in 2001. In addition, John contributed to various rural GP initiatives in Victoria and Australia, as well as to international initiatives through Wonca. John's participation in research and development projects was also wide-ranging, as demonstrated by the Study of Sustainable Models of Rural and Remote GP Services and the GP Workforce and Skills Minimum Dataset Project. His easy-going style, effective leadership and great networking abilities helped foster the Centre for Rural Health's development, particularly during the first decade.

Having worked as a draughtsman, Steve Kirkbright joined the Centre for Rural Health as a project officer and soon showed his strength in graphic design and use of communication information technology. Steve's contribution is evident in the full range of publications and audiovisual output up until he left Monash in 2006. Often Steve collaborated with Joe Hovel in Bendigo; Joe contributed to various projects drawing on his background in psychiatric nursing as well as his knowledge and expertise in information technology. Through the 1990s, Steve, Joe and John Togno helped to ensure that the Centre for Rural Health led the way in the use of communication technology to enhance our education, research and community development activities. From 1998, there was a formal information technology working group which enhanced many Centre for Rural Health projects, including the Rural Undergraduate Medical Placement System.

Dean Carson joined the centre as a research associate on the National Rural General Practice Study and stayed on for the Study of Sustainable Models of Rural and Remote GP Services and the GP Workforce and Skills Minimum Dataset Project. Dean's background in remote area demography and his practical approach to dealing with research challenges were invaluable contributors to the success of these projects.

Tutorial with Wildfire students 2003: Steve Kirkbright regularly taught communication and access to information skills to students and staff.

After a career in the ambulance service, Peter O'Meara joined the Centre for Rural Health as resources manager while undertaking his PhD through the University of New South Wales. In addition to his administrative role, Peter became involved in various projects and transferred in 1999 to the academic side of the centre. Peter's contribution included several Transforming Rural Urgent Care System projects, the Moe After Hours Medical Service and the Evaluation of the Alberton Project. Since completing his PhD, Peter has pursued a successful academic career and is now with La Trobe University in Bendigo.

When Peter O'Meara left, after the usual national advertising of the position was unsuccessful, we decided to take the unusual step of engaging an executive search firm to assist with recruitment. To our surprise, the head hunters found Rob Clough across the road from the Centre for Rural Health on the Latrobe Regional Health site at Gippsland Pathology. Rob brought his gentlemanly charm to the challenging, but essential role of keeping us all organised, and to balancing the books. This was no mean feat as the centre had grown quickly with numerous part-time clinical staff, as well as full-time academic and professional staff at multiple locations. In addition, Rob had the challenge of learning how the University expected things to be done, which did not always work in distributed rural settings.

From a nursing background, Mollie Burley joined the Centre for Rural Health as a research assistant. Over the years, Mollie was involved in many research and community projects including the Community Health and Health Promotion Program for Maffra and district, as well as various educational activities.

Anske Robinson brought her library background to the centre to assist with redevelopment of the Rural Health Research Register and stayed on contributing to many data-related projects including the Health Education Rural Remote Database, the Literature Information Service for Rural and Remote Health and the Victorian Rural Health Data Access Service which was known as Echidna. During her time with Monash, Anske studied part-time, first attaining her bachelors degree and ultimately her PhD.

Echidna was developed by Matthew McGrail who joined the centre as a research fellow and contributed his statistics expertise to many projects and activities. Subsequently, Matthew completed his PhD, supervised by John Humphreys, and has become a national leader in rural health workforce research.

Lauren Stephens was the only dietitian in the Latrobe Valley when she became one of the very early recruits to the centre. She was successful in implementing a project which educated GPs on nutrition and dietetics. Rather than reducing the need for dietitians, this project raised the doctors' awareness of the services that dietitians offer, and increased the demand. Subsequently, Lauren established a rural dietitians' network, and helped implement rural clinical placements for students in the Monash nutrition and dietetics program.

Janice Chesters came to the centre in 1998 fresh from completing her PhD. She quickly became a strong contributor to many educational, research and community activities including the Graduate Diploma/Master of Rural Health, Doctoring Towns: Narratives of Rural Practice, and the renewed and expanded secondary schools project, A Great Career Where You Live. Janice also travelled to Melbourne regularly to ensure that rural health would be well represented in the new five-year medical curriculum.

Raf Dua and Greg Beevor became known to us through their work on the project to build the new Latrobe Regional Hospital. With the development of regional clinical schools, there was a need to build new facilities which Raf and Greg coordinated in their inimitable style. Like the Latrobe Regional Hospital, all these projects were completed on time and within budget. In fact, Raf and Greg also provided assistance to me in the early years in Canada with planning and implementing development of the Northern Ontario School of Medicine.

Inspecting the new premises in Traralgon 1998: left to right – Roger Strasser, Lexia Bryant, Nick Saunders, Elaine Duffy, Peter O'Meara, Jo Wainer, John Pinnegar.

I had known Lexia Bryant when she was associate director of the Family Medicine Program in Victoria, and I was pleased to recruit her to the Centre for Rural Health in 1996. Lexia brought a passion for enhancing the quality of medical education, a commitment to the learners and an effective leadership style. She strengthened rural undergraduate initiatives including the rural GP mentor scheme, the rural students club, MURPA (Monash Undergraduate Research Projects Abroad) – later Wildfire – and rural health curriculum development for the new five-year medical course. In addition, Lexia worked with the Monash Department of General Practice and the University of Melbourne on the Victorian Advanced Training for General Practice, and collaborated with Jo Wainer on various research and education initiatives for women in rural practice. Lexia helped raise the national and international profile of Monash as a leader in rural health through her role as the second president of the Australian College of Rural and Remote Medicine, and as chair of the scientific program committee for the fifth Wonca World Rural Health Conference.

Di Wyatt came to the centre, after previous roles with the Victorian Government and as executive director of the Coordinating Unit for Rural Health Education in Victoria. With this background, Di was well placed to work with government on a range of health workforce activities and policy initiatives. She also took a major leadership role with the fifth Wonca World

Rural Health Conference and other Wonca initiatives. Subsequently, Di moved to Brisbane and became an important contributor to the development of the Australian College of Rural and Remote Medicine.

We could not and would not have functioned successfully without the dedicated work of many administrative and support staff. Julie Luke started as a receptionist and became an award-winning undergraduate student coordinator. Among the others were Joy Beckman, Paula Robinson, Kay Barrow, Michael Elswyk, Sarah Bamford, Sarah Evans, Heidi Robinson, Louise Bassam, Linda Kruger and Marg Bibic.

Achievements

By the time I left for Canada in 2002, Monash University was recognised as a national and international leader in rural health education and research. First the Centre, then the School of Rural Health, had pioneered a wide range of specific rural health education, workforce, research and community initiatives mentioned in the previous section, as well as multidisciplinary education for rural health practitioners and the double degree – Bachelor of Nursing/Bachelor of Rural Health Practice – which was designed to educate nurses prepared to practise in small communities.

In a real sense, we provided the prototype for subsequent Australian government programs including Rural Undergraduate Support and Coordination, University Departments of Rural Health, Rural Clinical Schools, and Regional Training Providers for regionalised GP training.

The Rural Undergraduate Support and Coordination Program, which was part of the GP Rural Incentives Program, provided $2.5 million per year for rural undergraduate medical education initiatives. Published in 1994, 'Rural doctors: Reforming undergraduate medical education for rural practice'[1] set out recommendations based on research evidence which showed that two major factors associated with entering rural practice after training are: a rural upbringing – that is, having grown up in a rural area – and positive clinical and educational experiences in the rural setting as part of undergraduate medical education. Medical schools were challenged to develop specific plans to achieve nine key targets for which they would receive ongoing funding subject to satisfactory annual reports. Within two years, all 10 medical schools in Australia at the time had signed on to the Rural Undergraduate Support and Coordination Program targets which included recruiting rural background medical students; ensuring that all students undertake a minimum of eight weeks clinical education in rural settings; and supporting rural practitioners as teachers and contributors to curriculum development.

University departments of rural health are academic units in rural or remote locations which have a multidisciplinary focus on public and Aboriginal health education and research. Monash's Centre for Rural Health provided a model for university departments of rural health, the first two of which were in the University of Sydney, Broken Hill, and the University of Queensland, Mt Isa. Subsequently, it was decided that each state should have a university department of rural health and the Victorian Government insisted on a collaborative model involving five universities which became the Victorian Universities Rural Health Consortium. The partners were Monash University, Gippsland; the University of Melbourne, Shepparton; La Trobe University, Bendigo; the University of Ballarat; and Deakin University, Warrnambool. The consortium facilitated networking of rural health initiatives across the state, including the secondary school program, A Great Career Where You Live.

Rural clinical schools have a focus on rural undergraduate medical education and research. Commonwealth Minister for Health, Dr Michael Wooldridge, came to Bairnsdale to launch the Rural Clinical Schools Program in 2001. Like the University Departments of Rural Health Program, the Rural Clinical Schools Program invests in rural academic infrastructure including purpose-built facilities and academic staff. In addition, the program provides funding to support the recruitment of rural background students and medical students undertaking clinical education in rural settings. Several medical schools have combined their university department of rural health and rural clinical school into a school of rural health following Monash University's lead.

In 1997–98, I was a member of the panel which undertook the Review of General Practice Training initiated by Minister Wooldridge. At his request, the panel recommended four options for the future. It was several years before the minister decided to establish General Practice Education and Training Ltd, which established contracts with regional training providers for general practice training along similar lines to the Gippsland Regional GP Training Program initiated by the Centre for Rural Health.

It is fair to say that the School of Rural Health has changed the perspective on universities of people living in rural and remote communities. Rather than being a distant ivory tower, the School of Rural Health is a local partner with hospitals, health services, and other community organisations. They work together to enhance retention and recruitment of health professionals and to improve the health status of the community. In this sense, the school thinks and acts locally, and has an impact at state, national and global levels.

For the last 10 years, I have been an occasional visitor to the school. I continue to be impressed by the commitment to improving rural health, and the spirit of innovation which are its hallmarks. The centre that began in 1992 as an idea which was ahead of its time, has continued through the first decade of the twenty-first century to set the trend in academic rural health for Australia and around the world.

Sarah and Roger Strasser 2001: 'Yes, Sarah, I have taken a job in Canada!'

Endnote

[1] Rural Undergraduate Steering Committee. 1994. 'Rural doctors: Reforming undergraduate medical education for rural practice'. Final report of the Rural Undergraduate Steering Committee for the Department of Human Services and Health. Canberra: Department of Human Services and Health.

CHAPTER 2

CHANGING EMPHASIS: MONASH UNIVERSITY DEPARTMENT OF RURAL AND INDIGENOUS HEALTH

The vision and key objectives of the Centre for Rural Health and the School of Rural Health have remained relatively constant over the last 20 years. The organisation has always been involved with medical education, including undergraduate, postgraduate and vocational training; academic and project research, and consultancy; rural development projects concentrating on connecting with rural communities; and workforce issues. The amount of time, money and effort spent on the various activity streams has varied significantly from one time to another, depending on funding, available expertise and opportunity.

Originally the centre's work was mainly undergraduate medical education. Although this activity continued, during the 1990s vocational training programs for general practitioners as well as research, community projects and consultancies comprised an increasing proportion of the organisation's output. At this time, the centre's workforce contained an eclectic mix of general practitioners and clinical teachers, other health professionals and sociologists. In the early 2000s elevation from centre to school status, development of Monash University's five-year medical curriculum, the introduction of the Commonwealth Government's Rural Clinical School Program and the subsequent establishment of the four regional clinical schools saw the primary focus return to undergraduate medical education. The burst of effort required to overcome this medical education hiatus was followed by many non-medically trained staff returning to their professional roots. The end result was the establishment of the Centre for Multi-Disciplinary Studies in Rural Health and later recognition of this centre as a bona fide university department of rural health: the Monash University Department of Rural and Indigenous Health.

Much is written elsewhere in this book of medical education and research. Here we look at the other streams of activity and the establishment of the Centre for Multi-Disciplinary Studies in Rural Health and Monash University Department of Rural and Indigenous Health. These other aspects of rural health, outside the mainstream academic disciplines, have been critical in the evolution of the school and fundamental to its culture. In many respects the activities in the Centre for Rural Health in the mid-1990s are most closely reflected in the activities of the University Department of Rural and Indigenous Health today.

A multidisciplinary focus

PROFESSOR ELAINE DUFFY

My first recollection of the Centre for Rural Health was July 1995 when I drove to Moe from Frankston to discuss with the renowned Professor Roger Strasser the potential for a one-year secondment to the centre from the then sub-faculty of Nursing. I thought that although the centre was young it was extremely vibrant and had unlimited potential to become a unique rural research and education centre within the medical faculty.

I found the centre physically small but the environment was full of energy, excitement and laughter blended with serious politics, academic work and critical scholarship. The place was buzzing despite the small space and the relatively small team. I had a great discussion with Roger and he agreed to my secondment to the centre for initially one year. As it turned out, I was at the centre for eight years. My time there was the most productive of my career in terms of successful grant writing, research performance, publications, conference presentations and professional involvement, thanks to the support provided to me by the staff and especially the mentoring I received from Roger. He was inspiring, creative, committed, energetic and a supreme champion for rural health. His political acumen was, and still is, outstanding.

The reputation of the centre, particularly in terms of rural research, was impressive. I was keen to develop rural nursing research and education as there had been minimal nursing contribution up to this point. The centre was expanding rapidly and achieved tremendous results by highlighting issues to rural health stakeholders, funding bodies and policy makers at local, state, national and international levels. At this time, rural health was a highly politicised priority for national and state governments. Under Roger's leadership the centre made the most of these opportunities, churning out submissions for projects and crucial project funding. It was exciting to be welcomed as part of this team.

In December 1996, after five years of extensive growth in budget, staff and function, a facilitated review planning workshop was held. A small group, to which Jo Wainer, Jane Greacen, Elaine Evans, Robert Hall and I belonged, was assigned the task of continuing the redevelopment process. The group was known as the group for organisational overview and development – the GOODies. We worked and played very well together. Robert Hall stimulated the team to think creatively with his astonishingly expansive and creative intellect. The result for the Centre for Rural Health was a three-dimensional matrix model that became the template for the future organisation. Before we implemented the new organisational structure, discussions in the faculty and the university were pointing toward the centre becoming the School of Rural Health, which it did in 2002.

The GOODies working on their strategic report 1997: left to right – Elaine Duffy, Robert Hall, Jo Wainer, Jane Greacen, Elaine Evans.

Though I represented the nursing discipline, a great number of projects and initiatives with which I was involved were multidisciplinary in nature. One of the more important initiatives in nursing, working in conjunction with the Monash School of Nursing at Churchill campus, was the development of a double degree in nursing and rural practice. The double degree was the result of national research that examined rural nursing practice and education. The project was undertaken in collaboration with Lesley Siegloff, a senior lecturer at La Trobe University at that time, and Mollie Burley. Mollie brought to the centre excellent skills in rural nursing, education and research.

Following 12 months of negotiations with and submissions to the Commonwealth Government, the Centre for Multi-Disciplinary Studies in Rural Health was established. This centre aimed to expand rural nursing and allied health education research, and to focus on Aboriginal health issues. The centre later became the Monash University Department of Rural and Indigenous Health. I worked with so many memorable characters at the Centre for Rural Health, but I would particularly like to acknowledge the work of Lexia Bryant, David Campbell, Peter O'Meara, Debra Cerasa, Anske Robinson and Matthew McGrail. My experience at the Centre for Rural Health was memorable, intellectually stimulating, challenging and great fun. It is one of the highlights of my career.

A wild idea in Gippsland

PROFESSOR PETER O'MEARA

My first association with the then Centre for Rural Health was in the mid-1990s in my role as a general manager in the Gippsland ambulance service. Contact had been made with Professor Roger Strasser to determine whether the Centre for Rural Health could help us recruit and retain ambulance service medical officers in the Gippsland region. Roger jumped at the opportunity to create a new role and to attract some sustainable income to the fledgling academic unit. This arrangement to provide medical officers persisted for a number of years until the absorption of rural and regional ambulance services into Ambulance Victoria.

Following an ambulance service restructure, I found myself at the centre as a part-time staff member undertaking a feasibility study on the establishment of an after-hours medical service in Moe following the closure of the local hospital. Both Roger Strasser and Dr Robert Hall were my key mentors on this study as I started my career transition from clinician/manager to academic. Like many of the early staff at the centre

I found myself undertaking a wide range of administrative, teaching and research activities. One of my early and most challenging assignments was to present the findings of a large research study concerning GP recruitment and retention at a rural health conference in Wagga Wagga. I was also interviewed on live regional radio within my first month of employment. I was quickly to discover that leaving my comfort zone would be a regular experience at the centre.

While the centre at that time was within the family of Monash University's Department of Community Medicine, there appeared to be a high degree of actual or implied autonomy from university policies and procedures. There existed a strong 'can do' culture that encouraged all staff to follow ideas and potential funding sources. Roger Strasser was particularly good at promoting our work and obtaining funding for projects from all levels of government and organisations that extended our short-term employment contracts for many years. My own involvement with the Moe After Hours Medical Service was sustained for five years from an initial three-month contract.

During the early days the centre consisted of a wide range of individuals drawn from the health professions, teaching, the social sciences and information technology. None of the staff had doctoral qualifications and by today's standards we were arguably operating on the very edge of our expertise and experience. All staff worked across projects and learnt a wide range of skills from each other. In my own case, I was fortunate to be able to learn many academic and technical skills from full-time staff such as Dean Carson and Steve Kirkbright who were driving forces in the early success of the Centre for Rural Health. Without Steve's efforts it is doubtful that any reports or promotional materials would ever have been created and followed through to completion. Out of necessity we became pioneers in marketing, interprofessional education, and research.

Over time this sense of collegiality transformed into a more strategic approach to personal and professional development; staff were encouraged and supported to undertake higher degrees, to write scholarly articles to further their own academic careers and to build rural health research capacity. A very successful venture in 2002 was the formation of a rural health writing group, predominately based in Gippsland, which produced strong scholarly outputs and helped launch a number of notable academic careers. The old centre gradually began to morph into a mainstream academic unit of Monash University.

Because of the diverse and dynamic nature of the research and evaluation activities being undertaken within the then School of Rural Health, it was often possible to combine project work with our doctoral and masters studies. I took advantage of this opportunity when I was 'rescued' from the role of resources manager to work on the Urgent Care in Small Rural Communities Project with Heather Kelly, Mollie Burley and others. From my perspective, this project was the catalyst for the beginning of my Australian and international academic collaborations.

Because of the limited office options in the new Traralgon building, a group of us found ourselves occupying the same work space where we shared ideas, frustrations, skills and many personal aspects of our lives. This multidisciplinary in-house group consisted of a couple of nurses, a statistician, a historian, a teacher, a paramedic and a library assistant. Others – including Kathy Pendergast and Phillippa Greene from East Gippsland and Janice Chesters, based locally – visited and collaborated with us in a constantly changing set of roles on projects that both challenged and stimulated us. The strength of this extended group was the support and encouragement we provided to each other as we grew and developed as researchers and people. Of that small group of research and writing collaborators at least five now have PhDs – Matthew McGrail, Claire Rickard, Anske Robinson, Rebecca Jones and I – while others completed masters degrees and published widely. Claire Rickard and I are now professors within our own disciplines, while others are making great strides in their ongoing academic careers.

To me, it is the success of these and other groups within the School of Rural Health that point to its predominance as a pioneering rural health academic unit which grew from little more than a rather wild idea in Gippsland.

Gaining recognition

DR JANICE CHESTERS

The internal business units of large organisations are generally fluid. They are subject to changes in managerial or organisational theory, and to the personalities and belief systems of leaders. Restructure and reorganisation are common, as is the refinement of internal relationships within the unit and of external duties and relationships with the wider organisation and the world. Units are restructured into larger or smaller sections, are joined or separated from larger units, or their reporting lines are changed. Units undertaking new or emerging business or undergoing rapid change are particularly prone to restructure or reorganisation. The School of Rural Health's change and development is both like every other organisation and yet totally unique and different from other similar groups.

The Monash University Centre for Rural Health was an early adopter of what was to become a major national program of rural health reform. The Department of Health and Ageing suggests that the groundwork for this rural health reform can be traced back to the first National Rural Health Conference held in 1991. The Centre for Rural Health was formed in 1992 and was the first rural health academic unit in Australia. The first major Commonwealth investment in rural health was a provision of the 1996–97 federal budget which funded the establishment of the University Departments of Rural Health Program. The centre was the model for this program; but, significantly, a university department of rural health at Monash was not recognised by the Commonwealth until much later, in 2006.

Why was the Centre for Rural Health not one of the first rural health academic units to receive university department of rural health funding? Many reasons have been offered over the years. They range from a reluctance to see rural Victoria as really rural to the fact that the centre already existed so could perhaps do without funding. Alternative theories involve intrigue and conspiracy, for instance, the thought that someone in power did not like the centre. Yet another possibility was the formation of the Victorian Universities Rural Health Consortium. It commenced in 1998 as a Commonwealth initiative to enhance the provision of education and training for rural and Aboriginal health professionals, as well as rural and Aboriginal workforce development and career planning. Perhaps the intention was to link all the universities involved in rural health into an organisation that was a little like a state-wide university department. The consortium was a troubled organisation and the Victorian Department of Human Services took over funding in 2002 after the Commonwealth withdrew. In turn, Victoria eventually pulled out of funding the consortium.

Funded or not, the Centre for Rural Health was committed to rural workforce development for all health disciplines. This is an important point to make. While the founding leader, Roger Strasser, was a medical doctor, the deputy director was a senior nurse, and staff members came from a variety of health and academic backgrounds. The centre was multidisciplinary from very early in its development. However, it could not be said to act as an interprofessional unit as the disciplines remained fairly firmly within their disciplinary silos. The centre continued to progress without Commonwealth funding, gaining some significant grant support from other sources, but seeing its Master of Rural Health program wax and wane. The centre was an independent unit within a changing faculty and university.

A defining moment for the centre occurred at a faculty meeting held in the lecture theatre – which later became the Strasser Auditorium – at Latrobe Regional Hospital. Most of the centre's staff was there to hear a presentation by the dean, Professor Nick Saunders, and Professor Chris Browne on the proposed faculty restructure. To us at the Centre for Rural Health it looked as though we were going to be part of a new School of Community Health. The centre, led by Roger Strasser, wanted to stay independent and become a School of Rural Health. At that meeting this looked like a very unlikely outcome. But then what became known as the Rural Clinical Schools Program was announced. This time Monash was among the first universities to be funded. In fact the whole program was formally launched at the brand new Bairnsdale Clinical School.

The Rural Clinical Schools Program was an important, well-funded program that changed the focus of the centre and provided a large enough income stream to justify school status. In 2000 the Centre for Rural Health became the School of Rural Health. The centre had always been involved in medical education but the rural clinical school funding increased the scale of our involvement manyfold. Coincidentally, the faculty was also undertaking a significant restructure of the medical curriculum at that time. Suddenly the majority of the school was involved in planning the medical curriculum right across the new five-year Monash course. From transition camp through to their final year, increasing numbers of Monash medical students were spending learning time in rural places.

The Rural Clinical Schools Program was a major undertaking that became the main game in the new School of Rural Health. This focus became dominant in part because Monash did not receive university department of rural health funding. That funding encouraged a more multidisciplinary focus that had been the dominant culture prior to clinical school funding. In yet another attempt to fund nursing and allied heath work, an application was made for Department of Health and Ageing funding. This time we were partially successful.

The Centre for Multi-Disciplinary Studies in Rural Health was funded by the department in 2002 for three years at $500,000 per annum. While the centre funding was significantly below that provided to university departments of rural health, it was a very significant first step along the pathway to acquiring full status as a university department of rural health.

Associate Professor Elaine Duffy was the first director of the Centre for Multi-Disciplinary Studies in Rural Health. The main thrust of this major research and education program came from the Traralgon school hub. However, fractional-time employees were located at all school sites including Bairnsdale, Mildura, and Bendigo. The centre undertook some key projects, one of which seemed to impact significantly on the attitudes of the Department of Health and Ageing toward the Monash School of Rural Health, eventually resulting in its gaining full status as a university department of rural health.

In 2005 the Centre for Multi-Disciplinary Studies in Rural Health's Indigenous Health Unit won a major Rural Undergraduate Support and Coordination Project of National Significance grant. As project leader, Monash partnered with the University of New South Wales and James Cook University to develop a recruitment model and material for Aboriginal students that could be used and applied by health science faculties across Australia. Led by Marlene Drysdale, what became known as the Footprints Project was very successful and well received by the Department of Health and Ageing. It was during one of many face-to-face reporting visits to Canberra that the questions of full university department of rural health status and, more importantly, funding, were raised.

One key meeting stood out in our minds. We were reporting yet again on Footprints, but were surprised to find an additional person in the room. The person said nothing for much of the meeting. Finally we were told that it was very likely that, should we apply, we would finally become a full university department of rural health. We asked about the time frame within which this would happen, whereupon the previously silent person replied, 'I suppose that you want it by next Monday.' We were meeting on a Friday. Although we were unsure of the spirit that this comment was made in, I recall we did say something like 'That would be great.'

MUDRIH did not start by Monday, but a full application was submitted by the head of school, Professor Geoff Solarsh, in May 2006. By June 2006 we were finally recognised as a full university department of rural health. Funding increased significantly and capital works funding was also made available. MUDRIH was now able to benefit from other national funding programs supporting work in rural pharmacy, mental health and research training. The number of staff grew and new senior roles were filled. This intense growth precipitated a move to the old head of school site in Moe. The Moe building became the fifth major site of the School of Rural Health. A small MUDRIH office at Monash's Clayton campus was also set up.

The Monash University Department of Rural and Indigenous Health continued to grow in strength between 2006 and 2010. We developed excellence in education – especially in Aboriginal health units – research training and rural placements in pharmacy, nursing, mental health and other allied health disciplines, and strong collaborative links with Latrobe Community Health Service. The team undertook research in a wide range of topics, especially mental health, interprofessional practice, Aboriginal health, and recruitment and retention. A focus on interprofessional practice replaced the more siloed focus on multidisciplinary work. The administrative and technical staff were excellent: they developed and updated the website, databases, student accommodation options, a conference room booking service, and offered high-level support to academic staff.

A gender perspective

DR JO WAINER, AM

The road trip to my job interview at the Monash University Centre for Rural Health in Moe was the leap of faith that characterises the first steps of the 'fool's journey'. Mystery was everywhere. The university, the centre, Gippsland, academic practice, and Moe were all unknown to me. As I drove along the highway I could feel my links with the familiar shredding. I was interviewed by Professor Roger Strasser and Dr Robert Hall in a scene of mutual incomprehension. I had two Monash medical faculty professors as referees and said I would move to Gippsland. That got me my first university job.

My initial role was modest. I was to take over and complete a study of the health needs of small rural communities. The best part was driving throughout Victoria to interview people in six communities, discovering that each community was different, as were people's views of health services.

My second task was to complete work for the Commonwealth: to understand how graduating female doctors could be attracted to rural practice. The driver was the shortage of rural doctors combined with the high male ratio in the rural medical workforce and the increasing ratio of graduating female doctors. The question was: what was needed so that women would go into rural practice? This question defined my role with the centre and absorbed me for the next decade.

After I had packed my bags, rented an old farmhouse and moved to Gippsland, I spent my first year at the Churchill campus of Monash University. I then moved to the Centre for Rural Health, based in an old ward at the Moe Hospital. Roger Strasser and his personal assistant, Elaine Evans, were the two full-time members of staff. Academic medical support was provided by GPs Dr Robert Hall and Dr Kaye Birks, and surgeon Mr David Birks. Others were gradually collected to support the work of the centre, which had two purposes: to understand how medical practice in rural environments was affected by those environments and, as a consequence, required specific models of training and care; to understand the drivers for doctors to go into rural practice.

Initially, the team was small enough for corridor conversations to provide a satisfactory organisational model. Roger's relentless drive to understand the relationship between place (rural) and function (medicine) attracted increasing funding and staff. There was the inevitable crunch when the goodwill model of management no longer worked. Associate Professor Elaine Duffy joined the team and under her guidance the next academic rural practice model was developed.

David Birks and I worked with a team we called the GOODies – the group for the organisational overview and development of the future management structure of the centre. David and I shared a working space, and the surgeon and the social scientist eventually found common ground. We recommended that the 'all roads lead to Roger' management practice devolve on to four teams, each with a team leader. I took on the role of team leader for the research team until Professor John Humphreys joined the centre and established the research office at Bendigo.

Early research into why some doctors practise in rural areas suggested that having a rural background and experiencing rural practice as an undergraduate were two key drivers. This was enough to encourage the Commonwealth Government to support medical faculties to include rural practice in their curriculum. Rural practice at the time was believed to be of a lesser standard than metropolitan medicine and of no interest to either the faculty or students. Roger worked tirelessly at faculty level to reverse this assumption, with spectacular success. Academic rural GP, Dr Lexia Bryant, worked out of tiny office spaces for years as the centre's representative at the faculty office at Clayton. Eventually she secured dedicated office space for the centre which hosted the rural students' club, visiting rural academics and full-time staff member, Teresa Neale, to coordinate rural requirements for students.

Staff at the centre began to organise placements for medical students with rural general practitioners. The faculty was encouraged, then funded and eventually required by the Commonwealth to provide some training in rural placements to all medical students and much training to some students.

Roger secured funding to build student accommodation and teaching facilities in the new Latrobe Regional Hospital in Traralgon. Rural doctors were recruited to teach and given honorary academic appointments, and the basis for the School of Rural Health was established.

I developed curriculum about women in rural practice as part of the project to encourage female students to consider a career as a rural doctor. This curriculum was taught by local female doctors including Kaye Birks, Jo McCubbin, Heather Hunter, Heather Miller, Sarah Strasser and Gillian Murray. The male medical students were difficult to engage with this topic so I expanded the curriculum into even more novel territory – gender and medicine – and recruited additional rural GPs such as Dr James Brown from Trafalgar to teach it.

I also wrote a proposal to faculty to put rural medicine on its priority list of strategically important research areas. The proposal both increased the profile of rural health research and opened up avenues of support within the faculty.

My major work with the centre and later the School of Rural Health was in understanding the way gender played out among rural doctors and, in particular, how to integrate women into the masculine culture of rural medicine. This was part academic – doing the research to understand what was going on – and part political – encouraging conversation where it mattered and establishing communities of interest. The major academic work was the development of the curriculum about gender and medicine. The work was published by the school as a monograph[1] and as a paper and chapter in *Women and Health*.[2]

This area was expanded through the work of my colleague, Dr Ann-Maree Nobelius, and included through the whole medical curriculum at Monash. I presented this work as a rural case study to the World Health Organisation forum of experts on gender and medicine in Geneva in 2006. Ann-Maree and I presented papers on teaching gender and medicine at world congresses on Gender Specific Medicine in Berlin and Stockholm. I presented the Monash gender and medicine curriculum at a UN forum[3] and as the keynote speaker at the Gender, Health and Medicine Conference in Taiwan in 2010. In 2012 I wrote the foreword and introduction to the international Handbook of Clinical Gender Medicine. So the small project that began as tutorials for medical students at Latrobe Regional Hospital morphed into the international conversation about gender and medicine.

The major research was a national study of rural doctors that explored how being female or male was reflected in satisfaction with rural practice. I found that predictors of years of future rural practice differed for men and women. As a staff member of the school I also undertook studies of female rural doctors and findings were presented to national and international rural conferences, published as monographs and as journal articles.[4]

I built on these studies to undertake a PhD exploring the relationship between medicine and the feminine. Dr George Somers and I were among the first PhD candidates with the school. Roger Strasser was my supervisor and when he left for Canada I transferred to the Alfred Psychiatry Research Unit, so did not graduate as a candidate from the school, although Dr Somers did.

Jo Wainer and Roger Strasser inspect a footpath pharmacy, most likely during the Wonca Rural Health Conference held in Durban in 2001.

The project of including women in rural practice was actively supported at the centre. Roger was visionary in his strategy of taking many of his staff to national and international conferences. I presented my work about female rural doctors at the World Organization of Family Doctors (Wonca) conferences, including the rural-specific ones, every year from 1998 to 2002. This included my involvement as a keynote speaker at the Calgary conference in Canada at which the Calgary Commitment to women family doctors was passed by the conference.[5] Sarah Strasser, Lexia Bryant and I were instrumental in writing that commitment.

My presentation on female rural doctors at the Durban Wonca rural congress in 1998 was the first time the topic had been considered at an international level. We made sure that women were included as both speakers and facilitators at all subsequent Wonca rural congresses, and eventually we developed the Wonca Rural Policy on Female Family Physicians in Rural Practice.[6] This was led by Dr Barbara Doty from Canada and was accepted as Wonca policy in 2003.[7]

Roger also encouraged Lexia Bryant to take on the task of including women in the foundation documents of the Australian College of Rural and Remote Medicine when that college was being formed. Lexia was able to draw on our work about female rural doctors, and subsequently became the chair of the women in rural practice committee that was established by the college; she later became president of the college.

Fostering collaboration

MOLLIE BURLEY

When I joined the Centre for Rural Health in 1992, it was a small centre with a strong medical and rural focus, involving researchers from nursing, psychology and education. In the years that followed, the centre changed names, roles and identities and finally became MUDRIH under the umbrella of the School of Rural Health. The roll-out of the Rural Clinical Schools Program changed the face of rural health in Victoria, as did the Jeff Kennett policies and closures from which health care has never recovered. During this time, what had by then become the School of Rural Health established four regional clinical schools and grew very quickly with an accompanying shift in focus to medical education. That left a gap in support for nursing and allied health – a gap Associate Professor Elaine Duffy and others sought to fill by establishing the Centre for Multi-Disciplinary Studies which focused on improving research, education and practice for nursing and allied health. It was within this environment that I worked on projects that aimed to effect concrete change at a local level – projects characterised by collaborative teams and relationships.

I began at the Centre for Rural Health as a research assistant working on the Small Rural Communities Project with Professor Roger Strasser, David

Harvey and other researchers from the Monash Churchill campus. After two years, I took a break from the centre and became involved in Victoria's development of nurse practitioners. It was as a member of the Victorian Department of Human Services nurse practitioner reference group that I first met Elaine Duffy.

Four years after leaving, I rejoined what was now the School of Rural Health to work with Heather Kelly and Peter O'Meara on the Urgent Care in Small Rural Communities Project. That project became Transforming Rural Urgent Care Systems. It resulted in the employment of a community ambulance officer in Mallacoota and an advanced practice nurse for the Mt Buller/Mt Stirling year-round health clinic.

My involvement with nursing practice continued on other projects. Phillippa Greene – a 'bush nurse' from Buchan – and I worked on the Quality Care in the Bush project and together we supported candidates seeking endorsement as nurse practitioners in Victoria. Following this project, our involvement in health professional education and training increased.

A Monash double degree in nursing and rural health was developed by a multidisciplinary team and included three MUDRIH units – rural communities, rural health policy and rural practice models – which were taught to nurses at Gippsland and Peninsula campuses and in Mildura. Around the same time Elaine Duffy and the head of nursing at Monash, Tony Barnett, negotiated with the Victorian Department of Human Services to co-deliver, via distance education, a unit in therapeutic medication management which was accepted for Victorian nurse practitioner endorsement. These course developments treated students as colleagues and used assessment methods more applicable to adult learning.

My involvement as program manager of another educational project led to my current interest in interprofessional collaboration. The SPECTRUM program (Support Program for Education and Clinical Training of Rural Undergraduates in Mildura) involved Mildura staff, including Dr John Russell, and 11 Mildura health and education agencies, and developed interprofessional collaboration educational material that is still used today.

MUDRIH's current interprofessional collaboration initiatives commenced in 2009 with the Building Capacity through Interprofessional Education Project. This project developed a student mapping model, a pre-workshop student video and an interprofessional collaboration workshop template and materials. At the same time we were working on the Extending Chronic Disease Management through Interprofessional Education Project.

All these initiatives involved working with local health agencies, and one of the closest relationships developed with Latrobe Community Health Services. MUDRIH established the Placement, Education and Research Unit to assist Latrobe Community Health Services to increase and improve student placements, and to facilitate education and research for staff using a capacity building model underpinned by interprofessional collaboration. Since the unit was established, 250 of the 400 Latrobe Community Health Services staff have participated in interprofessional collaboration programs and 32 student supervisors have been trained. Student placements have grown from 35 in 2009 – before the unit was set up – to 75 in 2010, and 151 in 2011. A research council has been formed with 16 active projects involving 27 staff.

With these experiences MUDRIH has also been able to establish much broader networks. Initially funded by MUDRIH, the Victorian Health and Social Care Interprofessional Network operated across Victoria and was subsequently funded by the Department of Human Services and Department of Health for another two years. The network organised a visit from Helena Low and Dawn Forman from the Centre for the Advancement of Interprofessional Education in the United Kingdom, which, following a suggestion from Dawn, eventually led me to form the Australasian Community of Interprofessional Collaborative Practice. The community includes representatives from academia and health services across Australia and New Zealand. These are people who operate at the health services coalface, who are actively engaged in delivering interprofessional collaboration programs, and who willingly share information and resources.

With support from head of school, Geoff Solarsh, and from Janice Chesters and Marlene Drysdale, I completed my masters degree in 2006. This was based on Part 2 of the Victorian Rural Nurse Project, Advanced Nursing Practice: A Bush Nursing Perspective, which was one of our early rural nursing projects. In turn, I have focused on supporting my colleagues and building structures and processes in all areas. Of course, buildings have made a difference, with the purpose-built Monash facility at Traralgon providing a fertile and productive working environment for my colleagues and me.

The story of MUDRIH's development is one of many people. Roger Strasser, Elaine Duffy and Geoff Solarsh were wonderful leaders and great supporters of MUDRIH in its various incarnations. The innovative Centre for Multi-Disciplinary Studies team included Claire Rickard, Heather Kelly, Vicki Dane based in Mildura, Janice Chesters, Marlene Drysdale, Phillippa Greene based in Bairnsdale, Matthew McGrail with administrative support from Michael Elswyk, Leanne Turnbull and Janelle McGrail. That team expanded into MUDRIH and now includes a variety of educators and researchers. The Indigenous Health Unit expanded and new mental health researchers joined the team.

Monash's internal and external changes have required us to adapt and identify new roles. Throughout, MUDRIH has provided wonderful opportunities for me to develop and grow professionally, and has enabled the development of lifelong friendships and networks. It has been a privilege to work with dedicated staff at MUDRIH and Latrobe Community Health Services as we strive to bridge the university/theory and practice/service gap.

Meeting in Moe 2005: left to right – Marlene Drysale, Matthew McGrail, Mollie Burlie, Anske Robinson.

Endnotes

1. Wainer, J; Bryant, L; Nobelius, A. 2002. 'Introducing gender perspectives into medical curricula'. Research Report. School of Rural Health, Monash University.
2. Wainer, J. 2003. 'Gender and the medical curriculum: A rural case study'. In *Teaching Gender, Teaching Women's Health: Case Studies in Medical and Health Sciences Education*, edited by Manderson, L. New York: Haworth Press.
3. 63rd UN Department of Public Information Non-Government Organisations Conference in Melbourne in 2010 at a workshop titled Incorporating Gender into Health Care and its Effect on Global Health and Achievement of the MDGs.

4   Wainer, J; Bryant, L; Strasser, R. 2001. 'Sustainable rural practice for female general practitioners'. *Australian Journal of Rural Health* 9 (Supplement 1, December): S43–S49.
Wainer, J; Carson, D; Strasser, R. 2000. 'Women and rural medical practice'. *South African Journal of Family Practice* 22 (6): 19–23.
Wainer, J; 2002. 'Women in the rural medical workforce'. Proceedings of Integration – Working Together for Rural Medicine: The Australian College of Rural and Remote Medicine Scientific Forum held jointly with the RWAV Victorian Rural General Practice Conference. April; Melbourne, Victoria: 24–26.
Wainer, J; Nobelius, A; Colville, D. 2002. 'A report on the experience of an international program in a gender perspective in medicine. Research Report. School of Rural Health, Monash University.
Wainer, J; Ginnane, J. 2001. 'It's where we live'. Report on the Victorian Female Rural Practitioner Survey. Melbourne: Rural Workforce Agency of Victoria.

5   Wonca Working Party on Rural Practice. 2000. 'Calgary commitment to women in rural family medical practice'. [Internet]. World Organisation of Family Doctors (Wonca). Accessed 28 May 2012. Available from: http://www.globalfamilydoctor.com/aboutWonca/working_groups/rural_training/rural_calgary_commitment.asp.

6   Wonca Working Party on Rural Practice. 2002. 'Policy for female physicians in rural practice'. [Internet]. World Organisation of Family Doctors (Wonca). Accessed 28 May 2012. Available from: http://www.globalfamilydoctor.com/aboutWonca/working_groups/rural_training/rural_Draft_Policy_for_Women_in_Rural_Practice.asp

7   Wonca Working Party on Rural Practice. 'Women in rural practice working group'. [Internet]. World Organisation of Family Doctors (Wonca). Accessed 28 May 2012. Available from: http://www.globalfamilydoctor.com/aboutWonca/working_groups/rural_training/rural_women_subgroup.asp

CHAPTER 3

EXTERNAL ENVIRONMENT: THE VIEW FROM THE OUTSIDE

An important factor in the creation and growth of the School of Rural Health has been its working relationships with key external stakeholders. Here we explore the environment in which the school has operated.

Michael Wooldridge sets the political scene that led to the introduction of key rural health initiatives. In so doing, he dismisses the idea – strongly held within the school – about why it did not receive University Departments of Rural Health funding in the initial round. Bob Wells and Di Wyatt speak from the perspective of Commonwealth and state health departments respectively, about their relationships with the school. The Victorian department funded many projects and provided some core funding that, in the early years, was the life's blood of the Centre for Rural Health; the Commonwealth's Rural Clinical Schools Program and University Departments of Rural Health Program are currently the school's major sources of funds. A perspective of the school and its place within the Faculty of Medicine, Nursing and Health Sciences at Monash is provided by Nick Saunders. Nick was dean of the faculty during a period of significant structural and curricular changes that also coincided with rapid growth for rural health at Monash. The chapter is concluded by Dane Huxley who speaks from his perspective as the chief executive officer at Mildura Base Hospital. Dane was a partner in the establishment of the Mildura Regional Clinical School on the hospital campus and elaborates on its effects.

Political reactions to rural problems

THE HON. DR MICHAEL WOOLDRIDGE

A number of rural health initiatives were introduced during my time as federal Minister for Health, including the John Flynn Scholarship Scheme,

University Departments of Rural Health and the Rural Clinical Schools Programs. These initiatives have had a profound impact on medical training, the provision of health services in rural and remote areas, and even the health of rural and regional townships themselves.

The policies have their origin prior to the 1996 election, when we were in opposition. I was of the view that, in a political sense, there had been a very substantial neglect of rural Australia. I believe that this was also a factor in the rise of Pauline Hanson. Following the election, within my portfolio, we set about addressing a number of issues aimed at making a difference to health care in rural Australia.

Our hard work resulted in a very deliberate strategy. In the period from 1975 to 1996, health had been a political graveyard for the coalition – we had been talking about health systems for 20 years and getting hammered. It was time to get the debate off health economics and on to everyday health issues that affect people. One of these issues was the acute shortage of medical practitioners in the country.

In 1996 the medical student intake was roughly 1200 with only 10 per cent of those coming from a rural or regional background; in some universities this was as low as 6 per cent. Research at the time suggested that only 5 per cent of the city origin students would go on to practise in a rural area, compared with 45 per cent of the rural-origin students.

I was also mindful that to spend time in a rural centre, in this era, was akin to committing academic and professional suicide. I wanted to change this dynamic by providing resources to rural areas. Dr Jack Best had performed some important intellectual and conceptual work that supported the view that the absence of rural infrastructure was a major impediment to attracting and retaining academics and professionals. Establishing infrastructure in rural communities also became an important and deliberate part of our strategy.

Our attention was initially caught by the public health unit in Broken Hill. This was small and modest, yet functioned quite well. This unit became the model for an initial proposal of six university departments of rural health. The number six would provide one for each state rather than one for each of the medical schools and was chosen very deliberately. We were not convinced that universities could be trusted to use the funding appropriately, so created some competitive tension. Another caveat was that the funding could not be spent on capital city campuses, to ensure that new buildings were not built on capital city campuses and merely dubbed 'University Department of Rural Health'.

Monash was initially unsuccessful. The people from Monash felt that they were being disadvantaged for already having the Centre for Rural Health.

Although we were concerned that the universities would not take up the concept and merely absorb the funding, the consensus within my department was that the University of Melbourne bid for Shepparton was a better proposition. This decision has been borne out in reviews of achievements at Shepparton. Similarly the University of Queensland missed out when the James Cook University/Deakin University bid for Mt Isa was successful. Neither James Cook nor Deakin had a medical school and the University of Queensland had assumed that they would be successful.

A major step was taken in 1998, largely in response to the Pauline Hanson phenomenon. The Prime Minister and others had decided that more effort was required on policies for rural Australia and ministers were invited to put forward suggestions. Around $2 billion per year of suggestions were provided with $300 million available. We had worked hard for two years and were able to refer to the advances made. For instance, there was now a full-time Professor of Medicine and Professor of Surgery located at Broken Hill. The Prime Minister and Deputy Prime Minister eventually decided that, rather than divide the available funds between portfolios, the lot should go to health, much to the chagrin of my colleagues.

My relationship with the universities was much stronger at this stage – they understood what I was on about. It was now time to make sure that every university had a chance to be involved.

Sharman Stone, member for Murray, and Peter McGauran, member for Gippsland deserve special mention. Both provided very strong advocacy for placing rural clinical schools in their regions. In fact, the Rural Clinical Schools initiative was announced in Bairnsdale, part of Peter's constituency, to highlight our intention to use this funding to place infrastructure directly into rural and regional towns.

My dealings with Monash during this time were primarily with the dean, Nick Saunders. Although I had little to do with Roger Strasser directly, people spoke to me highly of him and his work.

The Rural Clinical Schools Program has had a remarkable effect. Over 30 per cent of medical students are now recruited from rural areas, and a significant amount of the clinical training for medical undergraduates, both of rural and metropolitan origin, now occurs in rural locations. The program has also provided infrastructure and opportunities for joint appointments between health services and the universities that has attracted and retained professionals outside the capital cities. In many instances the clinical schools and their staff have had profound effects on the whole community, reversing lifetime trends.

RACGP training program Gippsland launch 1998: Roger Strasser (left) and Minister for Health, Michael Wooldridge (right).

I take some pride that the rural health initiatives that were introduced during my time as Minister for Health have proved to be significant and enduring. This did not happen by chance – there was no great momentum from around Australia for it to happen, and there was strong competition for the money. It does show how good policy can make an enormous difference. The policies that have changed the face of rural medicine in Australia have taken a very long time from concept to outcome. The challenge now is to apply the same attitude towards policy development to using the wonderful resources now available, to provide more postgraduate medical training outside the capital cities. The aim should be to ensure that our graduates have ahead of them a full range of options that are better integrated into state and regional health services.

A national template

ROBERT WELLS

I first became aware of, and began working with, the Monash University Centre for Rural Health in the early 1990s. I had just taken over as the head of the rural health policy division of the Commonwealth Department of Health and Ageing and, in collaboration with the states and various other bodies, worked on a national rural health strategy. Professor Roger Strasser and the Monash University Centre for Rural Health were heavily involved in this process.

I was impressed that this centre was the only academic unit looking at rural health and access issues from a rural setting, without initial government funding. Monash had set up the centre purely through its own undertaking. The centre was an innovation that provided a model for others to follow or challenge. It trained medical students in rural and primary care settings and, importantly, performed rural health research from a rural location. Monash University Centre for Rural Health was ahead of the game.

In the early 2000s the Rural Clinical School and University Departments of Rural Health Programs were introduced. The Centre for Rural Health in effect provided the template for later aims.

My department's dealings with the centre, and later school, were always most professional. There was never a shortage of good ideas from Professor Strasser and his colleagues, for which funding was required. In those days innovative thinking was required to tailor existing programs to fund rural concepts. Once funding was made available, the centre invariably succeeded in meeting the desired outcomes and worked openly and professionally with the department.

The early interactions with the Centre for Rural Health developed into an extremely strong and trusting relationship. This was particularly evident with the introduction of the Rural Clinical Schools project. This was an exciting new venture in which both the department and the universities learnt as we went. There was a sense of heading down a river at a quickening pace, not quite knowing what would be encountered round the next bend or where the next waterfall was situated. The relationship with the Monash school was open, positive and trusting; we were confident there were no possible problems being suppressed and did not doubt that the challenging objectives would be met.

The Rural Clinical School and University Departments of Rural Health Programs have been among the most innovative rural health initiatives introduced, not only in Australia but worldwide. These innovations required political vision and courage but can be traced back to the groundbreaking work of the Centre for Rural Health.

The state connection

DI WYATT

I first met Roger Strasser and became acquainted with the Monash University Centre for Rural Health in the early 1990s. Roger and I, in my capacity as manager of the Victorian Department of Human Services' rural health unit, were part of a national rural health strategy advisory group. The Centre for Rural Health was very new but was one of the key players and stakeholders in this field.

At the time there was a strong movement aimed at pressuring governments to address rural and remote health issues, and Roger and his centre were at the forefront. Significant time and effort was given to raising ideas, working with stakeholders, identifying issues and then developing policies and programs to deal with them. Headed by the world's first Professor of Rural Health, the Centre for Rural Health was uniquely placed to be a key contributor.

I recall that Professor John Humphreys was working with the Commonwealth, writing the Rural Health Strategy around this time, prior to joining the Centre for Rural Health. Many of the policies and programs emanating from this sector devolved to my department at state level, for implementation in partnership with the Centre for Rural Health. The relationship between the Victorian Department of Human Services – and in particular my boss, Ralph McLean – and the centre became crucial. Ralph relied upon and supported the centre. Funding was provided for many projects and some core funding was provided as well at this stage.

Wonca conference Melbourne 2002: Di Wyatt addresses the delegates.

Roger Strasser's drive and persistence were undeniable. He never tired of promoting rural health programs and ideas. For instance, his efforts were fundamental to the formation of the Coordinating Unit for Rural Health Education in Victoria program and the Rural Doctors Association of Victoria. Roger and the centre played important roles on many committees set up to implement government programs. Often they would come up with the ideas and implement them as well – all they needed was the funding! There is little doubt that the momentum built largely by Roger Strasser and the Centre for Rural Health provided the impetus for important federal programs such as the rural clinical schools and the university departments of rural health.

The Centre for Rural Health was also influential worldwide, particularly through its involvement with Wonca (the World Organization of National Colleges, Academies and Academic Associations of General Practitioners/Family Physicians). Roger served a term as chair of the working party on rural practice, a group that is still active to this day. Other universities around the world have since picked up the agenda, and centres for rural health have been formed based on the Centre for Rural Health and Roger Strasser's vision.

The Centre for Rural Health was a critical driver in the 1990s for gaining recognition of rural health issues and setting the national and international rural health agendas that are bearing fruit today.

Juggling expectations

EMERITUS PROFESSOR NICHOLAS SAUNDERS, AO

The end of the twentieth and the beginning of the twenty-first centuries were good years in which to be a dean of medicine interested in rural health, thanks to the policies and programs developed during that period by Dr Michael Wooldridge, the federal Minister for Health and Ageing, and his wily advisor, Jack Best.

Those two men were passionate about reducing disadvantage and improving the health of rural Australians. In large part, it was they who created the opportunity for medical schools and health faculties around the nation to create university departments of rural health and rural clinical schools, and to increase the proportion of medical students who came from rural and regional backgrounds. Generous funding provided by the federal government, for capital works and recurrent operating expenses, permitted the rapid expansion of teaching and research facilities, student accommodation, and clinical placements in rural and regional Australia. Substantial scholarship funds were also made available to support students who were willing to commit to spending at least the early part of their medical career in the bush.

When deans have plentiful resources at their disposal, effecting change is made much easier! Clearly, some politics were involved as the schemes were rolled out. Why, for example, was the Monash rural clinical school officially named the Bairnsdale Rural Clinical School and launched in that delightful East Gippsland town by Minister Wooldridge, when most of the school's activities were to be located elsewhere in Victoria, if not to bolster the local member's electoral prospects? And it was burdensome having to keep university department of rural health and rural clinical school funding strictly siloed because of the needs of the Canberra bureaucracy. But the programs that Michael Wooldridge and Jack Best initiated have been a resounding success overall, as judged by the large number of students who have gained a meaningful rural experience as part of their undergraduate program, the resultant internationally significant innovation in teaching programs, and the growth of high quality rural clinical services over the last two decades.

During this time Monash's Faculty of Medicine, Nursing and Health Sciences also benefited from initiatives implemented in rural Victoria by the Kennett and Bracks governments. Particularly noteworthy events for Monash were the opening of the Latrobe Regional Hospital and a significant expansion and upgrade of Bendigo Health Care Group. This investment by the Victorian Government greatly improved the opportunity for a broadly-based clinical education in rural Victoria and made the prospect of a rural career in the health professions much more attractive.

The substantial increase in resources for medical schools to build their rural programs during the late 1990s and early 2000s allowed the recruitment of talented staff from around the world. For example, the head of Monash's School of Rural Health, Professor Geoff Solarsh, was recruited from the University of Natal in South Africa, and the director of the University of Melbourne's program in Shepparton, Professor Dawn de Witt, was recruited from the University of Washington in the United States. People like Geoff and Dawn brought their experience and new ideas to rural and regional Australia which benefited our students and enriched the community.

Nick Saunders, dean of faculty, opens the new facilities at Latrobe Regional Hospital, Traralgon 1998.

As might be expected in any organisation during a time of rapid expansion, the new federal University Department of Rural Health and Rural Clinical School Programs caused some 'growing pains' in the faculty.

Outside the School of Rural Health, some staff were envious of the very generous funding provided by the federal health department for rurally-based medical education; on a per capita basis, it was roughly four times greater than the funding provided by the federal education department! Some staff were upset that rural clinical school funding was strictly tied to medical students and could not be used to support nursing and allied health students in rural settings, especially as the funding of these disciplines was already far less than that of medicine. Others, particularly those in the biological sciences, expressed concern that the teaching focus of funding might diminish the faculty's research reputation through the appointment of staff without a strong track record in research. A significant number wondered aloud whether the quality of teaching and the student experience in a rural setting would match that in the city and particularly, whether experience heavily based in general practice would be as effective as specialty-based tertiary referral hospital experience. Concerns were also expressed about being able to adequately support a widely distributed faculty, notwithstanding recent developments in electronic communication.

My job as dean was to listen carefully to these concerns, assist the leadership of the School of Rural Health to formulate strategies to address them, communicate with the faculty leadership about the intended approach, and support the school in its efforts.

Inside the School of Rural Health, there was a sense of great excitement and an urgency to grasp the opportunities brought by a major increase in resources. However, the growth and diversification of staffing and the expansion of activities outside Gippsland also created challenges. The Centre for Rural Health had suddenly become the School of Rural Health and, as a consequence, expectations of its performance in teaching and research had increased considerably. Many staff were not adequately prepared to meet these new expectations, particularly in research. The school's centre of gravity was seen by some members as having shifted too far north-west, with attendant anxiety about the fate of the Gippsland site. The need to expand the numbers of medically qualified staff in the school brought the problems of recruitment to rural Australia into sharp focus and was seen by some members as a threat to the multidisciplinary culture of the previous centre. There was also concern that the growth of specialist staff numbers might threaten the centre's strong commitment to primary care.

Here, my job was to work with the staff of the school to build their belief and confidence that change would bring rewards to them, individually and collectively, and to Monash and the community. The recruitment of several senior academic leaders from a variety of disciplines including, importantly, the social sciences, greatly assisted the transition.

The successful resolution of these significant challenges demonstrates the willingness of staff at Monash to work together and to be innovative in their approach to solving problems. It also points to the faculty's strong commitment to equity for disadvantaged groups, in education and health, and to excellence in teaching, research and community service. As the Centre for Rural Health has grown and diversified to become a fully fledged school within a vibrant faculty, it has made a very real contribution to the lives of rural Victorians and to the multidisciplinary scholarship of rural health, nationally and internationally.

It was a great privilege to serve as dean of the Faculty of Medicine, Nursing and Health Sciences at Monash between 1998 and 2003. The opportunity to assist in the development of the School of Rural Health provided me with one of the most rewarding experiences of my professional life.

Working together for mutual benefit

DANE HUXLEY

The turn of the century was a time of great change at Mildura Base Hospital. As part of the sweeping reforms introduced by the Kennett state government we had become Victoria's second privately owned public hospital. We operated from a brand new hospital built on a greenfield site. The infrastructure was owned by the Motor Trades Association of Australia and the service was provided by Ramsay Healthcare. This made for a complicated three-way contract agreement between the state government's Department of Human Services, the Motor Traders Association and Ramsay Health Care.

I first became aware that Monash University was considering placing a clinical school in Mildura when I was approached by its dean of medicine, Professor Nick Saunders. We were enthusiastic about the prospect and believed that recognition as a teaching hospital would enhance our reputation and standing. It appeared that the project would be of mutual benefit to our respective organisations. Nick was very impressive and his amicable style quickly moved negotiations onto a heads of agreement.

It was agreed that Monash would build the clinical school – consisting of teaching rooms, academic and administration offices and accommodation for students – on the hospital campus. The clinical school buildings would become part of the hospital buildings on completion. The Department of Human Services and the other parties to the contract were all in agreement, so the decision was made to start the construction while it was left to the lawyers to work through the contractual arrangements. The smoothness of the original negotiations and agreement with Nick Saunders was a stark contrast to the difficulties encountered with the contract variations. The buildings were complete and in use for many months before the contracts were finalised. Yet even through this episode, the trusting relationship between Mildura Base Hospital and Monash was maintained as both organisations were determined to make it work and to be as good as their word.

The relationship developed further as the clinical school became established and the students commenced. The clinical school director, Dr John Russell, was a pleasure to work with. The mutual trust that had developed, and still exists, meant that there have been very few issues between our organisations, and when any have arisen they have been resolved without fuss.

The presence of the students around the hospital has had a noticeable effect. The patients enjoy them and their interest in the patients' health, while the hospital staff have also reacted positively. A state of enhanced learning and sharing of knowledge has resulted and benefited both staff and students. I know that some of the students placed in Mildura in the early days had academic and social concerns. I also know that the vast majority of students have completed their placements and returned to Melbourne with glowing reports of their experiences, both clinical and social.

The facilities that the clinical school has built are excellent and have become a resource for the hospital and staff. The meeting and lecture rooms, complete with audiovisual equipment, are available for hospital use, while the state-of-art clinical simulation centre is a boon for all health professionals in the region.

While the presence of the clinical school has not made a quantifiable difference to the recruitment of health professionals to the region, it has had more subtle effects. A number of past and present clinical school staff have held joint appointments with the hospital and other health service organisations in the region. In fact, John Russell worked for many years as director of emergency services at the hospital in concert with his Monash role. The school provides the opportunity for doctors and other health professionals to teach or mentor students, which can be a welcome distraction from full-time clinical service.

The opportunity exists for further joint appointments between the clinical school and hospital in Mildura. In the future all the hospital's training could occur at the clinical school. Jointly appointed positions would centralise training that has previously been performed sporadically across both organisations and provide exciting career options for those with the appropriate skills.

From the point of view of the Mildura Base Hospital, the establishment of a Mildura Regional Clinical School has been an unqualified success. Monash has always been a delight to deal with. This has been exemplified in the past by Nick Saunders and John Russell, and presently by Associate Professor Fiona Wright, the current director. They have nurtured the relationship that has seen our organisations work together for mutual benefit.

Inspecting the progress of construction in Mildura 2003: left to right – Robert Clough, Elaine Duffy, John Russell.

CHAPTER 4

RURAL MEDICAL TRAINING: APPLYING THE CURRICULUM IN A RURAL ENVIRONMENT

As Roger Strasser wrote in the opening chapter, much of the impetus for the establishment of the Centre for Rural Health came from recognition that the rural doctor shortage problem began at, or before, medical school. The fact that fewer medical students came from rural areas was compounded by the poor standing in which rural practice was held by city-based senior medical school teachers, and the lack of exposure to rural practice for students in the clinical years of their training.

In this chapter John Togno tells of the early rural placements for medical students and the evolution of these over time. John was head of the education stream within the school and was very active in incorporating rural placements and issues into Monash's five-year medical curriculum. David Campbell is another long-time rural medical educator who writes of the establishment of the East Gippsland Regional Clinical School, the philosophies behind it and his passion for the merits of rural practice. Gordon Whyte was the inaugural director of the Bendigo Regional Clinical School and was involved in curriculum planning and implementation within the faculty before returning as head of school. Gordon writes of his experiences in setting up the regional clinical school and the curriculum issues he encountered. The final product is reviewed, from a student perspective, by Ryan Spencer, Elyssia Bourke and John Clark.

Positive exposure to rural practice

DR JOHN TOGNO

The objective of rural medical placements in both the old six-year curriculum and the development of the current five-year curriculum has been very straightforward: that rural clinical placements should contribute to the teaching and learning of medical students by giving them a positive exposure to clinical experiences in the rural setting, therefore aiming to develop and stimulate a longer term career interest in rural medicine.

There have been rural placements in the medical curriculum at Monash for many years. These placements date back to the mid-1970s. At this time the then recently established Department of General Practice – with the newly appointed Dr, later Professor, John Murtagh as a strong advocate of rural medicine – had a six-week block of teaching in the final year of the undergraduate curriculum. Part of this six-week block was a two-week placement with a rural GP. It was a genuine immersion experience, with medical students shadowing their rural GPs in and after hours, doing hospital rounds and theatre lists and often sharing the house of the GP and their family during their placement. The rural experience was a markedly different experience for many students compared to their metropolitan placements.

From the late 1970s onwards, urban GPs were beginning to lose many of their clinical skill sets to the rapidly growing number of specialists setting up their practices in suburban areas. In contrast, rural GPs then – as now – provided a diverse range of procedural skills to their communities; in addition, they provided the comprehensive range of non-procedural clinical skills required to manage complex medical conditions in the rural areas of Victoria where they were working. For many students, whose clinical education until then had been in tertiary hospitals – where they encountered about 3 per cent of all clinical presentations and specialists' openly expressed bias against the skill sets of GPs – this was a truly eye-opening exposure to a style of clinical practice that they could not otherwise have encountered or comprehended.

For many students this rural placement was an experiential epiphany that led them to a career path as a rural GP, or at least to a deeper understanding of the key role that GPs provide in the delivery of health care to the other 97 per cent of the population. For others, it was possibly a more traumatic psychological experience. Some experienced the displacement anxiety of their first prolonged excursion alone outside a major metropolitan setting. Cognitive disruption resulted from the direct observation of clinical skills and procedures that were being practised well outside what students had been indoctrinated to perceive as the safety of a major clinical precinct such as the Alfred Hospital in Melbourne.

In time, this two-week rural GP placement, which was in later years delivered by the Centre for Rural Health in association with the Department of General Practice, became one of the most highly rated teaching and learning experiences in the six-year medical undergraduate curriculum.

Another medical placement in the six-year curriculum that played an important role in the development of the Centre for Rural Health – not least because of the $300 payment that went with every student – was the delivery of the rural-based electives for Year 2 and 3 medical students. At that stage of the course all medical students had to undertake a faculty-approved elective experience which was not directly linked to their core teaching and learning. Often such electives were offered by the pre-clinical departments in the medical faculty on campus and therefore were a slight variation on the laboratory or small teaching room approach usually offered to the students; there were also several relatively innovative electives offered both within the medical faculty and other faculties on the Clayton campus – especially the arts faculty.

Few if any of these metropolitan-based electives had any clinical or patient contact components. The advantage that the centre had was the ability to leverage the wide range of rural-based clinical teachers associated with the centre to offer a range of electives that gave the students direct clinical exposure. From the relatively modest beginning of Alpine electives first set up by Dr Sarah Strasser, the range of electives offered by the centre expanded to include attachments at the Bendigo Primary Care Clinic and direct observation of rural proceduralists coordinated by me. All of these electives were, out of necessity, offered outside the usual curriculum teaching hours, but the lure of 'hands-on' clinical experience meant that giving up holidays or weekend time was no barrier for the students in comparison to the experiences offered by the Clayton-based academics.

Of the final cohorts in the six-year curriculum, just under 50 per cent of all Year 2 and 3 medical students chose a rural elective, an achievement that was for other academics in the faculty, whether they realised it or not, a harbinger of the future impact the School of Rural Health would have on the distribution of students across the teaching sites on offer.

The current model for rural medical placements was built on these successful foundations. As is the case for many other Australian medical school students, Monash medical students now have an extended immersion-like experience during their rural GP placements. In these placements, they continue to see a wider scope of clinical practice delivered by rural GPs than by their metropolitan counterparts. Overall, this style of placement continues to offer a positive exposure for students that actively demonstrates to them the benefits of taking up a career as a GP – especially as a rural GP: career satisfaction and the development of competence in delivering an extended range of procedural and non-procedural skills. In the first two clinical years of the five-year curriculum, students frequently reported their positive anecdotal experiences with clinical exposure compared with those of their metropolitan peers.

Has the overall objective of promoting rural medicine as a career, by offering a positive rural clinical placement, been achieved? In some ways it is still too early to give a definitive judgment. To date, early career choices by Monash medical students who have been through the School of Rural Health's new curriculum have not shown a promising degree of uptake in rural-based careers. However, it may be 10 years or more – that is, after the completion of their postgraduate vocational training – before the outcomes can be judged; only when practitioners choose locations where they will spend a significant time in clinical practice can the success or failure of rural exposure for students finally be determined.

There are number of people who have profoundly influenced the evolution of rural health at Monash. Roger Strasser was not only the founder, but the original convert to rural health. Neil Carson and John Murtagh were important because they had faith in Roger's ability to develop the Centre for Rural Health into what it has become, and supported him to do so. Marlene Drysdale fought and won the fight for inclusion of increased Aboriginal health perspectives into the medical curriculum. David Campbell and John Russell provided the clinical leadership that promoted and protected rural issues when under attack from metropolitan forces. The rural general practitioners, who selflessly and repeatedly made themselves available as clinical teachers, have been critical to the success of the program. Among others, Amanda Young and Janice Chesters have influenced the creation of a school of rural health as opposed to a school of rural medicine. And finally, all the administration staff have been crucial because without them none of this would have happened.

Clinical training in East Gippsland

ASSOCIATE PROFESSOR DAVID CAMPBELL

The evolution of the Centre for Rural Health and then the School of Rural Health can be seen from a number of perspectives. I would like to provide the perhaps 'peripheral' perspective of a rural GP in East Gippsland, at one end of the school's geographical footprint. I underwent a very gradual involvement with the Centre for Rural Health in the first decade of this 20-year period that developed into a much more significant leadership role in the second decade.

My first involvement with the centre occurred in the early 1990s, when Roger Strasser, then 'a GP from Moe', was travelling around Gippsland canvassing support for the establishment of a regional GP training program in Gippsland. On the face of it, the purpose of Roger's visit to Lakes Entrance was to enlist practices to accept registrars into the Royal Australian College of General Practitioners Family Medicine Program. Of course this was the first step in Roger's plan to establish an independent regional training program in Gippsland, which evolved into the first such regional program in the country. This was a significant move away from the traditional centrally-managed program 'rotating registrars out' to rural practices. Roger's concept was to provide the means by which doctors training for general practice could undertake all their training in a rural placement.

The legacy of Roger's approach has been significant. In Australia we have had a fully regionalised GP training program for the past decade. We now have a popular and well-funded national program supporting pre-vocational doctors to experience rural general practice before they embark on specialist or GP training. And in Gippsland we have a network of practices with a strong culture of education which has formed the basis of the Rural Clinical School Program, involving placement of medical students in general practice.

It would be a mistake to assume these developments have been a result of serendipity or perception of a 'greenfields' opportunity. The early days of the Centre for Rural Health were characterised by a strong reliance on research, with policy and programs developed on the basis of available evidence. Rural workforce was at the centre of this evidence base, with much of local, state and national policy arising from the Australian and international research which demonstrated that health practitioners were more likely to choose a rural career firstly if they were of rural origin, and secondly if they had a positive rural experience as part of their training.

As a result of this research, early Centre for Rural Health activities included: a network of support for GP teachers hosting short-term student placements from the University of Melbourne and Monash University medical schools; a Monash rural mentor scheme linking students interested in rural practice with experienced rural GPs; a rural secondary schools program to improve recruitment of rural students into medical training; and a rural students' club – which evolved into Wildfire – supporting medical students with an interest in rural practice. At the same time, the centre began to exert increasing influence on the Monash medical curriculum.

Much of the centre's development in the 1990s both contributed to, and was the beneficiary of, significant policy change at a national level. In March 2000, Dr Jack Best released his 'Rural Health Stocktake Advisory Paper', and among the recommendations arising from this work was the concept of a national network of rurally-based medical school programs. This was the catalyst for the development of the Rural Clinical School Program.

By that time, the Monash School of Rural Health had expanded from the original Centre for Rural Health site at Moe to include campuses at Traralgon, Bendigo and Mildura. In late 2000, universities with medical schools were invited to apply for funding under the proposed Rural Clinical School Program. Monash University's submission initially included rural clinical school sites at Traralgon, Bendigo and Mildura. Such was the political importance of this new program at the time that Monash was invited by the government to include in its application an additional regional clinical school with campuses in East Gippsland – at Bairnsdale and Sale. As a result, on 6 February 2001, the federal Minister for Health, Dr Michael Wooldridge, came to Bairnsdale to officially launch the national Rural Clinical School Program.

The East Gippsland Regional Clinical School proposal was based on the successful rural community curriculum model developed by Flinders University in South Australia. This involved placement of Year 4 students in rural general practice for the full academic year, providing the opportunity for students to immerse themselves in a rural town, with clinical supervision from rural clinicians, including visiting specialists. The East Gippsland program also included placement of Year 3 students, studying medicine and surgery, for the full year at Central Gippsland Health Service in Sale.

Following almost two years of planning and infrastructure development, five Year 3 students commenced in Sale in 2004. In 2005 nine students were placed in practices in Bairnsdale, Lakes Entrance and Orbost to undertake Year 4. This was significant in several ways. It was the first venture by the Monash medicine program into a fully-integrated, rural community GP-based curriculum program. It was a significant deviation from the traditional short clinical rotations through specialist-led tertiary hospital placements in the disciplines delivered in Year 4. This program 'immersed' students in a rural community, as they worked in a practice and lived as part of the local community for a full year.

David Campbell, Director East Gippsland Regional Clinical School (left) and John Russell, Director Mildura Regional Clinical School (right) at a rural expo in 2006. Rural expos were held annually to 'sell' rural placements to medical students.

The East Gippsland Year 4 program has been regularly evaluated since its inception. This has involved an annual program review incorporating student and preceptor feedback, and monthly local faculty meetings, with representation from each of the practices and other local clinicians teaching in the program, to discuss progress. The student cohort meets with the program coordinators on a weekly basis to discuss progress, curriculum issues and clinical experiences. The program underwent a major external comparative evaluation with the Flinders University Parallel Rural Community Curriculum in 2010, and a series of publications has arisen from this evaluation.

Curriculum delivery for the Year 4 program has been based on self-directed adult learning principles. Students have opportunities to undertake clinical activity in general practices, in the local hospital maternity ward and in the emergency department. They benefit from a rostered rotation through both local and visiting specialist clinics and hospital attendance relevant to the learning objectives of the curriculum. In addition, students have been encouraged to keep a log book of clinical activities, including clinical and procedural skills demonstrated outside the requirements of the curriculum.

Students have regularly and repeatedly reported that the breadth of clinical opportunities involved in the program and the large number of clinical encounters involving one-to-one supervision from an experienced rural clinician, provide a strong and valuable learning experience.

Year 4 students have undertaken identical summative assessments to those of their peers in the 'traditional' central program based in Clayton. The only variation has been the timing of some semester-based summative assessments, given the nature of the integrated year-long program. Students have performed as well as or better than their peers in the traditional metropolitan-based Year 4 program.

In 2010 the program was expanded to include a similar cohort of students in and around the Sale area, supported from the Sale campus of the East Gippsland Regional Clinical School based at Central Gippsland Health Service. This involved placement of students in practices in Sale, Maffra, Heyfield and Yarram, under an identical model to that of the Bairnsdale program. At this stage, the student cohort also included Year C students from the graduate entry Gippsland Medical School, undertaking a clinical year program identical to the Year 4 program of the undergraduate five-year medicine course at Clayton. The program has continued to offer year-long placements for students in Years 3 and 4 of the central program and Years B and C of the Gippsland Medical School program, with combined Year 4C and Year 3B cohorts respectively.

Participating practices have been supported with infrastructure funding from the Rural Clinical School Program, as well as an annual teaching payment to the GP teachers. This has enabled the students to have access to their own consulting room and close clinical supervision under a 'parallel consulting' model.

Engagement with the local communities in the towns in which the students are placed has been a strong feature of the program. This has been facilitated by an active regional community advisory committee, made up of local community leaders and representatives from local and state government, service clubs, and other local educational bodies. This committee has provided the impetus for the establishment of the East Gippsland Student Scholarship, available to local-origin students undertaking medicine with Monash, to assist them through their early university studies. Their local communities have provided the following supports: assistance with part-time employment; involvement in sporting, music and drama clubs; and local health education activities.

Students' knowledge of Aboriginal health issues has increased with the assistance of short-term placements in local Aboriginal medical services. In addition, East Gippsland Regional Clinical School has been very active in supporting the East Gippsland Aboriginal community via the establishment of the East Gippsland School for Aboriginal Health Professionals, led by local Aboriginal community leaders. This initiative has been developed to identify the support young Aboriginals need to embark on careers in health care through enrolment in tertiary studies. In 2012, we have funded a research officer for 12 months to undertake research with the local community to identify these support requirements.

Expansion of the program has progressed steadily over the past decade, with additions to the school buildings at both the Sale and Bairnsdale campuses. As of 2012, East Gippsland hosts 30 full-time students in the Year 3B and Year 4C programs; students are placed in hospitals and practices from Sale and Heyfield in central Gippsland, to Omeo in the east. In addition, the program hosts groups of Year 1, 2 and 5D students for shorter placements, providing these students with the opportunity to understand the nature of rural communities and their health services.

In 2012, the $1.5 million extensions to the East Gippsland Regional Clinical School campus based within the grounds of Bairnsdale Regional Health Service were officially opened. The extensions included:

- enlargement and improvement of the Bairnsdale Regional Health Service hospital library
- enlargement of office space for Bairnsdale Regional Health Service Nursing Education Unit
- enlargement of the current clinical skills/simulation suite and creation of a separate clinical skills/simulation suite for the Monash Gippsland School of Nursing program
- an extra eight academic offices to accommodate the Monash Gippsland School of Nursing program and the School of Rural Health program

- two extra tutorial rooms to accommodate the School of Nursing program, as well as extra administration offices and meeting rooms
- two offices for research staff supporting the East Gippsland School for Aboriginal Health Professionals
- a large family meeting room for family members of hospital inpatients.

These improvements were in addition to the expansion of the Sale campus in 2011, with provision for a large, fully-equipped simulation suite and extra academic space.

In 2011, the Bairnsdale campus commenced delivery of the Monash Gippsland School of Nursing program, and in 2012 there are 28 School of Nursing students undertaking Year 2 and 3 of the nursing degree, based entirely in and around Bairnsdale. This allows for local residents, including students bridging from the East Gippsland TAFE Division 2 nursing program, to continue their studies locally without the need to travel to Monash's Churchill campus.

The program will also continue to build on current support activities of for: intern training at Bairnsdale Regional Health Service; practice nurse education within local general practices; and paramedic training with Ambulance Victoria. The program will be enhanced with the recently-acquired grant of $480,000 from Health Workforce Australia, through the Gippsland Clinical Placement Network, to support simulation-based education in East Gippsland.

We have also developed a strong research program with two full-time research officers based in Bairnsdale. They support local and regional research projects, including the evaluation of our interdisciplinary education programs. The establishment and strengthening of academic leadership has been an essential component of the East Gippsland programs. This has involved recruiting local clinicians and providing academic support and recognition, based on a long-term strategy of succession planning and sustainability.

Finally, we have developed significant international strategic relationships with rural medical education programs in New Zealand with the University of Otago, and in South Africa with the University of Witswatersrand, as well as maintaining an ongoing close relationship with Roger Strasser at the Northern Ontario School of Medicine in Canada.

The East Gippsland Regional Clinical School has now become an integral and readily-identifiable part of the East Gippsland community. The school provides opportunities for local clinicians to receive support and recognition for teaching activities in medicine, nursing and allied health education. There is an enhanced rate of clinician retention and more opportunities for students in these disciplines to undertake their training as members of the local community which supports them. Already we are seeing the results of this program in workforce terms, with previous students returning to undertake further studies and providing health care for the community.

The regional clinical school stands as testament to the success of the Rural Clinical School Program. It provides a working example of how the infrastructure of a rural clinical school, and the presence of academic and administrative staff, can be used to support all levels of medical and health education, including continued professional development for local clinicians. Rural clinical schools can also become a focus of support for the recruitment of local community members into health professional training, with consequent benefits for the community at many levels.

Two universities meet in Bendigo

PROFESSOR GORDON WHYTE

In June 2001, I was appointed to the exciting new position of interim director of the proposed new regional clinical school at Bendigo under the School of Rural Health. The appointment was within the Bendigo Health Care Group (Bendigo Health) but funded from Monash University.

Bendigo Health was taking all its interns and registrars on rotation from the Austin Hospital. It also took 12 University of Melbourne medical students on six-week rotations from the Austin for general medical and surgical experience. The University of Melbourne had a School of Rural Health based in Shepparton and Wangaratta. So a Monash link for Bendigo was seen by some as somewhat anomalous, given its comprehensive academic footprint in Gippsland. Monash became involved at Bendigo Health primarily due to a shared vision between Professor Nick Saunders, dean of medicine at Monash, and Kathy Byrne, CEO of Bendigo Health. I had the impression that the University of Melbourne students from the Austin did not value the rural experience.

My task at Bendigo was to identify, coordinate and plan the financial and skill resources, and to provide leadership to prepare for the construction of physical facilities in the new calendar year, in readiness for the following year's medical students.

The first steps were to understand the new five-year curriculum being developed at Monash in Clayton and how the School of Rural Health was intending to expand from its base around Professor Roger Strasser at Traralgon. I also had to understand the new concepts of dispersed medical education. The consultant staff at Bendigo Health were ambivalent about teaching medical students. Some consultants saw the medical school as an opportunity to enhance their own enjoyment of medicine; others saw it as a recruitment base for residents and registrars; and yet others thought it would be a drain on an already busy life. The hospital was also concerned about the potential inefficiencies and distractions that teaching students might entail. Dr Chris Holmes, Dr John Togno and I met with Professor Paul Worley of the Riverland program and Professor Sandy Reid of the Wagga Wagga pilot scheme to understand dispersed medical education in a general practice setting. Professor Chris Browne at Monash was already working with John Togno and Janice Chesters to ensure that rural issues were embedded in the new curriculum. Adding further to the complexity, the structures that had evolved around Roger Strasser were subsequently complicated by his departure for Canada.

The most pressing problem was to find accommodation for the expected 70-odd students as well as the professional and academic staff. Our initial home was a vacant shop shared with Sandra Barrie (administration), Graham Allardice (manager) and Andrew Moon (information technology). Following initial suggestions by John Togno, the building that had formerly been the Northern District School of Nursing (and, more recently, the regional office of the Victorian Department of Health) was purchased. However, when negotiations eventually matured, the timeline was very tight. The excellent facilities on Rowan St became Monash property for about $1 million but needed significant renovation to make them useable and comfortable. The site was large enough to become a hub for medical organisations in Bendigo (including the regional GP training network as well as our own research and academic staff) for many years. However, it was physically just over a kilometre from the hospital – a chronic problem for students after a heavy night! Land was purchased between the acute and chronic care campuses of Bendigo Health in Mercy Street, and a lecture theatre, library and tutorial rooms were constructed on this site. These buildings and their recent expansion have provided a major contribution towards the sustainability of health professionals in the Loddon Mallee region.

In June 2002, I was appointed as professor/director of the Bendigo Regional Clinical School. I reported to Monash for academic issues and to Bendigo Health for clinical issues. On any one day I might be in the role of registrar in the emergency department, staff specialist on the wards or laboratory, or professor in the Monash role. Our first Monash students were expected in February 2004 for Year 3 experience in a general hospital. Meanwhile, the University of Melbourne had changed its course; its clinical year started in June, with the first of six problem-based learning style clinical rotations. These were designed for large teaching hospitals, but allowed a way to spread the Monash and University of Melbourne students through the hospital without having both groups of students in one place at the same time. The University of Melbourne blocks that overlapped with Monash units were:

- endocrine, renal, urology and vascular surgery
- cardiorespiratory medicine and surgery, and general medicine
- neurosciences, ophthalmology, and ear, nose and throat
- haematology, oncology and infectious diseases
- emergency medicine, perioperative care, orthopaedics and rheumatology
- gastrointestinal medicine and surgery, and general surgery.

Pathophysiology, radiology, professional development, legal medicine and evidence-based medicine were separate, parallel programs for each university and were taught continuously through the year. This meant that we could accommodate the two universities and their student rotations without overloading any one ward. However, the tutors had to keep changing between the problem-based learning set for each university, which were of rather different styles. The students were also different: University of Melbourne students focused on facts and exams, whereas Monash students wanted to explore ideas and were not too fussed about not knowing a detail which could be looked up.

In 2002 and 2003, Monash was still finalising its Year 3 problem-based learning sets and structures. In fact, one of the first curricular plans was totally unworkable. Essentially, a six-year course of three pre-clinical and three clinical years had been compressed to two and a half years of each, so that in Year 3 all Monash students would be on the wards for the second half of the year and none in the first half of the year. The dean, Professor Steve Wesslingh, and I came up with a modification that was eventually adopted so that students spent the whole of their third year in a clinical setting. However, Monash had planned to deal with head and neck anatomy and with pharmacology in the first half of Year 3, so the first few batches of students needed remediation in those areas to bring them up to speed. The disaffection of the Monash pharmacology department and the dispersed delivery of teaching meant that we waited a long time for adequate pharmacology resources.

The 36 University of Melbourne problem-based learning sets and another 36 tutorials could be fairly neatly categorised around each of the six blocks mentioned previously. However, Monash had 30 clinically-based and 33 problem-based cases to discuss which did not neatly fit into the six categories. The disease conditions broadly coincided. In addition, it was impossible to make the clinically-based cases real because of the unpredictability of patient availability for a particular condition on a particular week. Bendigo staff contributed to and strongly shaped the Monash problem-based learning curriculum as well as pushing continuously for access to good pathology tutorials to support the Bendigo pathologists. Radiology tutorials were always excellent and we recruited various outside teachers to help with pharmacology and anatomy. We were well supported in law, professional development and evidence-based medicine. We were able to appoint Professor Peter Disler in geriatrics, and Associate Professor Beth Penington in surgery, to senior academic appointments at Bendigo Health, to the benefit of both organisations.

The transition went smoothly and students were enthusiastic about their Bendigo experience in 2004 and 2005. In fact the reputation of rural training exceeded our capacity to handle the applications. The Bendigo community advisory committee was an enthusiastic supporter of the school, providing simulated patients, a grand mayoral reception for students and invitations to dinner. The students responded by joining local clubs and activities. They did well in their exams, and the academic and professional staff were justifiably proud of their achievement. The hospital had been concerned that the inefficiencies introduced by teaching students were not built into its base funding, and it mounted an argument that this issue should be recognised financially by the government. In due course, an increment was built into funding to match the grants received by the large metropolitan teaching hospitals.

Plans were finalised for the 2005 Year 4 rural students to gain their experience in children's health, women's health, psychiatry and general practice. Bendigo is excellently staffed in children's health and women's health and there was enthusiastic support to take students. Professor Fiona Judd and her department provided excellent psychiatry teaching, despite being somewhat understaffed. General practices in Castlemaine, Bendigo and Kerang provided wonderful hands-on experiences for our students, and that group has subsequently been expanded and supported by a much more sophisticated IT network than when we started.

In 2004, Professor Geoff Solarsh arrived to take over the head of school role which Professor John Humphreys and I had carried since the departure of Professor Elaine Duffy. At this stage there were, including myself, five professors at Bendigo: Geoff Solarsh, John Humphreys, Peter Disler and Fiona Judd, and Beth Penington as an associate professor. All teaching staff had appointments as lecturers or senior lecturers and Chris Holmes has subsequently been appointed as clinical associate professor.

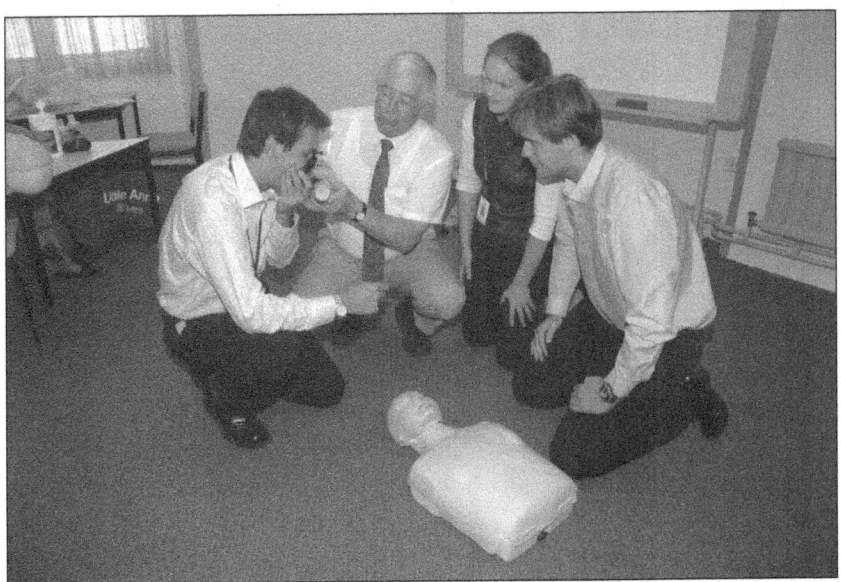

Gordon Whyte provides clinical training to Bendigo-based students in 2005.

In 2006 a new tranche of funds had been made available and Monash had successfully bid for the graduate entry Gippsland Medical School and the Northern Victoria Regional Medical Education Network (NVRMEN) coalition with the University of Melbourne across northern Victoria. With Malaysia clinical teaching coming on line as well, Monash was suddenly faced with a quantum leap in management complexity for its clinical years. For students to be placed in the Monash regional clinical schools they had to commit, at the time of their enrolment, to the NVRMEN model or as graduates to Gippsland Medical School. This also meant that metropolitan students could not access rural teaching or subsequent recruitment into rural postgraduate positions. Boundary issues between Gippsland Medical School and School of Rural Health sites in Gippsland became acute. Under these environmental changes, the school began to fragment and lose its momentum and sense of common purpose. With the head of school based in Bendigo, the Gippsland-based clinical schools felt abandoned. Mildura Regional Clinical School also felt dominated by decisions being taken in Bendigo. Finally, the University of Melbourne was also changing to a new model of medical education and was placing great importance on the intellectual property of its clinical curriculum and control of its students, making life difficult between the NVRMEN partners.

The response of the dean, Professor Steve Wesselingh, and Geoff Solarsh was to ask me to take over as interim head of school, effective from January 2008. The position was subsequently converted into head of school from mid-2009, allowing Geoff to focus on NVRMEN. The combination of my central role in the curricular aspects of medical education and my role as head of school, allowed the School of Rural Health to continue to place its stamp on the curriculum. The other outcome was to identify and address IT connectivity issues which, in the end, also required a central Monash restructure to give proper leadership across the University. I saw my two and a half years as mostly interim head of school as a difficult change-management program. The development of relationships between Gippsland Medical School and the Gippsland and East Gippsland Regional Clinical Schools required careful nurturing. The Monash University Department of Rural and Indigenous Health continued to evolve as it struggled to establish itself. This evolution also required continued support and direction from the head of school during this time. I was proud of the School of Rural Health I passed to Professor Judi Walker when she took over as head of school at the end of 2010.

This has been a wonderful journey for the Monash School of Rural Health and for myself at Bendigo, in Sharjah, and as head of school with a central role in curriculum. The school has been instrumental in substantially increasing the intellectual and social capital of health services in rural Victoria. Interns and registrars want to return to rural and regional settings thus reflecting the changed perceptions of rural health as the place to be. Nick Saunders's riding instructions when we set out on this journey were 'to build so that Bendigo Health could not conceive of itself without Monash University'. I think we have achieved an excellent foundation for that outcome. We have built a unique rural clinical school; it is the most complex and complete in Australia, now poised to lead the world in rural health education and research.

Returning to rural

DR RYAN SPENCER

I came to university from the country and intended to return there. Imagine my delight on discovering a whole university department largely dedicated to ensuring that I did so. The Monash University School of Rural Health and its student-run rural health club, Wildfire, became a home away from home for me during the early years of university. Although Monash's Clayton campus had once been surrounded by paddocks, it is now well and truly part of the concrete jungle that is Melbourne's urban sprawl. I was soon spending as much time at the School of Rural Health's new Clayton office, complete with Wildfire office and the ever-bubbly Teresa Neale, as I was in Monash's lecture theatres.

Towards the end of our first year I was surprised but delighted to be elected the new Wildfire president, from which began my connection with the School of Rural Health. Among the obligatory barbecues and ice-cream days, I was also invited to help organise the rural placements for Monash's 'new' medical curriculum. Dr John Togno was keen to get a student's perspective and thus regularly sought advice from me and other Wildfire committee members, often through informal chats in the Wildfire office.

Such 'stakeholder consultation' is rarely done well but John's openness to our concerns and suggestions – and lots of work by many in the school – led to such a successful roll-out the following year that the school was required to introduce a selection process due to the rural placements' overwhelming popularity.

Our year in Bendigo was a fantastic experience, both clinically and socially. On the clinical side we were enthusiastically taught by both local doctors and patients. One particularly memorable experience involved a fellow Year 3 student being taught how to examine the respiratory system by the patient he was supposed to be examining! 'Oh dear,' she said as he began the examination by listening to the lungs with his stethoscope, 'they usually start with the hands.' Being a smaller hospital it seemed that almost all the clinical staff were involved in teaching us in some way.

Space was at a premium and 'tute' groups were small, meaning that there was nowhere to hide from tricky questions from senior medical staff. Nowhere was this more evident than in the legendary tutes with the local ophthalmologist. Another major advantage of the Bendigo placement was the travel time to Friday morning problem-based learning tutes. No urban clinical student could wake up at 7:55 am, walk down a flight of stairs in pyjamas and moccasins and be early for their tute on the ground floor.

While having the student accommodation and tute rooms on separate floors of the recently renovated Lister House was great for the morning commute, it meant the staff offices were also on the ground floor. Thankfully, apart from an issue with the heating – which led to the top floor being a balmy 28 degrees most of the year – this never caused any trouble. Instead it fostered a better relationship between students and staff, and led to many combined social events throughout the year. Many other social events occurred without staff as they were unable to keep up with the hectic social calendar – described by some of them as one year-long party! Nonetheless, everyone passed – and most with improved marks compared with previous years – and thus it was time to move on.

In 2005 the small group I had met at Wildfire moved to far-east Gippsland for another clinical year in the country. Again, engaging clinical experiences and dedicated School of Rural Health staff marked the year, this time in the picturesque setting of Lakes Entrance. As we were out of the reach of – and largely forgotten by – the University bureaucracy back at Clayton, we got on with learning medicine. The system must have worked as the end of the year saw good exam results for all and signalled the end of my association with the school as a student. It was time to spend some time in the city.

Like any organisation, the School of Rural Health is only as good as its staff. It has been an amazing experience to be educated and guided by and, more recently, to collaborate with such a dedicated group of people.

The School of Rural Health's first 20 years of success, like all successes, has been built on personal relationships, both between staff members and between staff and students. The challenge for the future is maintaining these relationships among an incredible increase in student – and therefore staff – numbers. Making students feel more than a number was once a major strength of the rural clinical schools. Maintaining this point of difference from the urban clinical schools will be significantly challenging, with the shine of the new program gone and overwhelming numbers of students entering the school's various clinical programs. Future research success relies similarly on fostering relationships and supporting collaborations across the wide geographical and interprofessional landscape of the school. The issues around rural health have changed over the last 20 years, but the importance of the school's role in both education and research is stronger than ever. It will be fascinating to see what the next 20 years bring.

Not for the faint-hearted

JOHN CLARK

For a country high school student, entry to medicine was a daunting idea. The numbers of students applying, scores required for entry, and expectations were ominous. A new program called the Extended Rural Cohort had just begun for medical students, offering greater length of clinical training in regional and rural Victoria. Joining the Extended Rural Cohort was not for the faint-hearted, with a two-and-a-half-year commitment to stay in the country, but it had an adventure-like appeal. Growing up in rural Victoria, I knew that, yes, there was still electricity and running water outside Melbourne and that I did not have to hunt for my dinner! However, a number of surprises and learning experiences were in store.

Being part of a medical team in a rural hospital forced us to step up both our professional and clinical skills from day one. We went from a group of 300 students in Melbourne, to just 12 in Mildura. Not only did we stand out when we first arrived, with our fresh faces and sometimes disorientated air in the hospital; we also stood out even more if we were not on time for early-morning ward rounds. It was not long, though, before we were adopted by the staff, and the ladies in the cafeteria were giving us an excessive number of chocolate freckles to have with our morning coffee! We also found ourselves writing up the notes, ordering investigations and admitting patients to the hospital in a very short space of time.

The staff got to know our skills and capabilities which was an amazing advantage, considering that many of our city peers needed to re-introduce themselves to a new team every week. Our advantage began in Year 3 with writing medical notes and inserting cannulas, and built up to Year 4 when doctors were confident enough in us to sign off on the more complex management plans we had written. During our placements in the country we spent time in a variety of health services and groups. On numerous occasions I would coincidentally refer a general practice patient to myself as the 'apprentice paediatric resident' and see them later at the hospital clinic. Similarly, women I would see for final antenatal checks in general practice would before long be breathing through contractions in the labour ward, and we would be delivering the baby with an experienced assistant. This continuity was unique to our rural experience.

Even closer was our relationship with the clinical school staff. In Mildura, the whole clinical school team would partake in *The Age* superquiz. We would be stocked up with farm produce, courtesy of Kate, the lovely student administrator, who even gave private golf lessons on request. Being 600 km from Melbourne, we immersed ourselves in town life, joining the gym and netball team, working at the pool, playing in the orchestra and attending opening nights of exhibitions at Art Vault – a gallery run by a local surgeon's wife. We also found our own fun, hosting our own first birthday party, Halloween and a progressive formal dinner through our homes in the town. Phenomenally, almost every student maintained some kind of student leadership role despite being so far from the rest of the student body in Clayton.

The chance to build relationships with patients in rural communities was challenging and rewarding. In a general practice in Woodend, we performed our own consultations, checking our plans off with the supervising doctors at the end. In one of these consultations I met a teenage girl who came in with her mother; the daughter wanted to begin taking the oral contraceptive pill. Using the skills we had learnt through our women's health study, I completed a history and examination and recommended a pill based on the needs of the patient. I then gave a summary of this to the GP, who was happy with my reasoning. Everything about the visit appeared to be routine, which was why I was surprised when our receptionist pulled me aside that afternoon to ask what had happened with the patient. I was initially worried that I had done something wrong and that a complaint had been made, but my fears were soon dismissed. The family wanted my name so that they could come back for appointments in the future. The receptionist then explained that before going into the room, the girl's mother had been upset that they had to see a medical student – despite the consent process in place – yet I had completely changed their attitude in the 30 minutes I had spent with them. I do not believe I am an exceptional student, but rather that instances such as this are possible due to the immersion experience of the rural clinical schools.

We learnt how living in these communities had an impact on the medical services that could be provided, and we discovered the reasons patients present to health services. This also had an impact on the types of medical problems that emerged; for instance, cellulitis – a bacterial skin infection – was highly prevalent in visiting fruit pickers in Mildura; they worked with bare legs and feet, would get scratches, and then go swimming in the Murray River. Knowing when, why and how patients present to their GP or to hospital is a valuable skill to have as a doctor; this was something we were able to quickly discover in the rural clinical schools.

Even now in Melbourne, the rural clinical school experience is still having an impact on our learning and understanding of medical practice. I am currently completing a medical science honours year with the intensive care unit at the Royal Children's Hospital. Our team runs the Paediatric Emergency Transfer Service (PETS), bringing the sickest children in Victoria to hospital. I have now been at both the sending and receiving ends of this service and, more often than not, know the referring doctor and the services and skills available in the town from which the child is referred. Being given a state-wide context for health care delivery has been an incredible experience and one that I believe will make our new medical graduates outstanding in their field.

Welcoming patients

ELYSSIA BOURKE

In my five years as a student with the School of Rural Health, I have spent many hours on placement at sites all around Victoria, as well as being involved with the student rural health club, Wildfire. This connection has been one of the most important and rewarding throughout my time as a medical student.

I am an Extended Rural Cohort student hailing from Cardigan, near Ballarat. I spent two years in Clayton, completed my Year 3 placement in Mildura, and in Year 4 I completed six months of general practice in Gisborne and six months of specialty placements in Bendigo.

For me, the most rewarding part of undertaking my medical placements in these regional and rural areas has been the patients. It may be a generalisation, but patients in these regional and rural areas are really welcoming. Every single patient I encountered opened up not only their medical history to me, but also their personal history.

From pregnant mothers to men with testicular lumps, to people with drug addiction problems, patients knew that I was a training doctor and were more than willing to let me in on their consultations and their lives. Some of the personal details that people shared with me during those times had not even been shared with their close friends and family, and some had not shared this information with anyone. To have that level of trust placed in me was a very humbling experience. I learnt so much thanks to those amazing people – even though many of them probably did not realise it. I hope in the future I can give back to them some of what they gave to me.

The second thing that I have noticed in rural clinical sites is the incredible selflessness of the clinical school staff. I do not know what I would have done without Jenny Timmis and Kate Murdoch in Mildura when things went wrong, or when I needed a mum away from home! Likewise, having a cup of tea with Carole Meade in Woodend was often the highlight of our academic week and a great chance to get much-needed advice and de-stress.

One of the greatest experiences that I had during my time as a medical student on placement was my mentor week with Dr Cullen, local obstetrician and gynaecologist in Bendigo. The mentor week consisted of shadowing my allocated doctor. Wherever he went, I went – even if this was to a birth at 2 am! This meant doing everything from assisting with caesareans at the private hospital in Bendigo to watching IVF, to sitting in with gynaecological consults in Echuca. This was an amazing experience and has seriously made me consider obstetrics and gynaecology as a potential career path – something I never thought I would do!

Another memorable experience was the time that I spent in general practice and the amount of autonomy I was given as a student during that placement. Being able to see patients independently, organise scripts and pathology slips for the doctor to sign, and counsel patients regarding results they had received was really rewarding. I felt like I was actually a practising doctor! I always looked forward to my days in general practice – even when it was in Rochester, an hour's drive from Bendigo, because I knew that those days were going to be interesting and that I would always have to use my clinical reasoning skills. In other rotations that is usually done by the senior doctors.

The teaching culture at the regional clinical schools is remarkable. Clinical school staff and hospital staff are all available and willing to teach students everything and anything. The number of hours spent in tutorials – both scheduled and impromptu – was extensive. The smaller class sizes were most helpful, especially because all the students knew each other so well that the phrase 'no such thing as a dumb question' really rang true. Everyone supported one another and this created a great environment for learning. I also have to commend the dedication of the teaching staff at the sites where I was based – they were awesome, especially when tutes were conducted at 4–7 pm over their dinner time and arguably during some of the best TV viewing.

Without a doubt I will look back on these years as some of the best experiences of my life. The people I have met, the things I have learnt and the amazing friendships I have made have been incredible. The School of

Rural Health is arguably the greatest addition to the medical faculty. People do not realise how good the clinical experiences are in these areas until they have done the course themselves. I owe a lot to the School of Rural Health – so thank you, and happy twentieth anniversary!

CHAPTER 5

COLLABORATION IN NORTHERN VICTORIA: EMBEDDING EDUCATION IN REGIONAL HEALTH SERVICES AND COMMUNITIES

PROFESSOR GEOFF SOLARSH

A mere 10 years ago, the only trace of Monash University activity in the Loddon Mallee region were a small and struggling primary care clinic in a slightly dilapidated weatherboard building opposite the Bendigo Hospital, and a fledgling Centre for Rural Mental Health, recently established as a joint venture between the School of Psychiatry and Psychology at Monash and Bendigo Health.

Today, in mid-2012, the Monash School of Rural Health occupies large and well-appointed clinical schools on the regional hospital campuses in Bendigo and Mildura. Our Bendigo Regional Clinical School is an integral part of a new health education and research precinct shared with the La Trobe University Rural Health School and the Bendigo Primary Care Centre. Bendigo is the Monash hub of the NVRMEN (Northern Victoria Regional Medical Education Network), a collaborative innovation in medical education with the University of Melbourne that places over 200 medical students each year in north-west Victorian educational sites. Bendigo is also the La Trobe University hub for a regional education program for large numbers of students from nursing, allied health and dentistry within the same geographical footprint. Together these three universities, with their many health service partners and distributed rural communities, constitute a major health workforce intervention; they sustain the supply of health professionals from all disciplines and improve health status in these and other rural and remote communities in Australia.

Foundations

Rural clinical schools

The NVRMEN story has its start in 2001 with the federal funding of rural clinical schools in Australia. These schools provided the infrastructure and support for the placement and education of medical students in regional, rural and remote health services and communities. A condition of this funding was that all participating medical schools must place at least 25 per cent of their government-funded students – the vast majority of students at most universities – in these rural schools for at least one of the clinical years of the medical course. By selectively enrolling students from rural communities and by returning them to the same or similar communities for prolonged periods of education during their formative clinical years, it was expected that a good number of these students would return to practise in these areas after their graduation. This expectation was largely based on published evidence from rural medical education programs in other countries. The rural clinical school strategy provides an opportunity, on an unprecedented national scale, to apply these principles and to reproduce these results in Australian rural settings.

The Monash School of Rural Health

Between 2001 and 2002 Monash established four regional clinical schools, two in Mildura and Bendigo in the Loddon Mallee region in north-west Victoria, and two in Traralgon and Bairnsdale in the Gippsland region in south-east Victoria. These four schools, in their respective sub-regions, proceeded to recruit local health service providers in hospitals, general practices and other health agencies as key partners and future placement venues for their students. They also began to recruit and appoint small teams of clinical tutors and administrators to work with the central faculty to design and run rural medical education programs that were fully aligned with the Monash medical curriculum while, at the same time, providing essential rural context and content. Together with their staff and multiple health services and community partners, these four regional clinical schools provided the initial configuration for the Monash School of Rural Health.

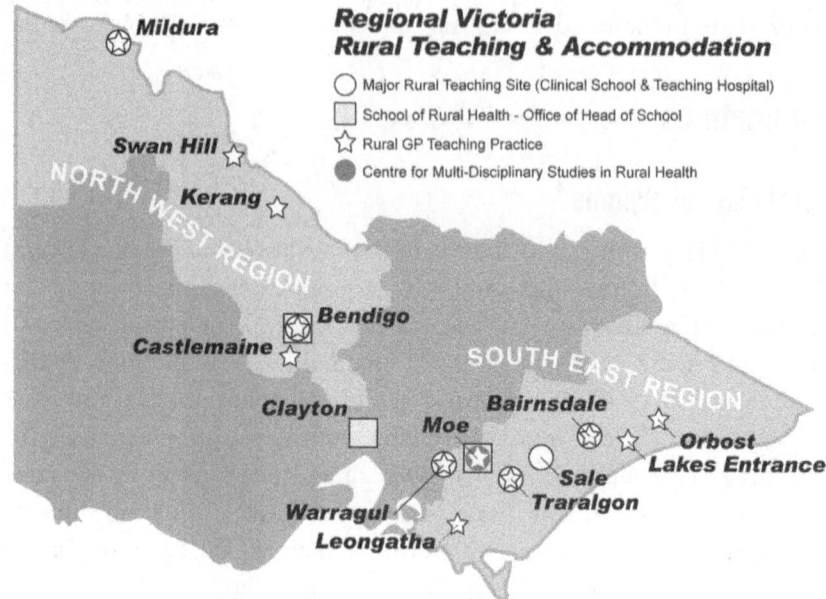

School of Rural Health teaching sites in 2006.

The first cohort of clinical students entered the Monash School of Rural Health in 2004 in the first clinical year – Year 3 – of the medical course. By the end of 2006 the school, at all its sites, had demonstrated its capacity to successfully place students in all three clinical years – Years 3 to 5 – to meet all their respective learning objectives in rural settings and to achieve assessment results that were at least equivalent to those achieved in metropolitan clinical schools. The Monash School of Rural Health had passed its initial viability test and was, with its counterparts elsewhere in Australia, considered to be fully launched as part of a national innovation in medical education and health workforce development.

The School of Rural Health was the overarching governance structure for all rural programs and activities at Monash, including: the regional clinical schools; the Centre for Multi-Disciplinary Studies in Rural Health – soon to become the Monash University Department of Rural and Indigenous Health; a whole-of-school rural research program; and many smaller rural projects and programs over the school's entire footprint. As a formally constituted school in the Faculty of Medicine, Nursing and Health Sciences, it had the same status, privileges and obligations as all other schools in the faculty.

Expansion of medical education programs in Australia

In 2006, after much discussion and analysis, the dominant view in universities, professional colleges and government was that Australia faced a medical and health workforce crisis. Its reliance on overseas-trained medical graduates was neither viable as a future health workforce strategy nor morally defensible, given the parlous state of health services in donor countries. Faced with this reality and a clear federal commitment to fund a national expansion of medical training, the state government in Victoria announced the creation of 220 new medical training places. Proposals were quickly received and approved for Deakin University to set up a new graduate entry medical school in western Victoria with 120 places, centred on Geelong, and for Monash to set up a new graduate entry medical school in Gippsland with 40 places, centred on its existing Gippsland campus. The remaining 60 places in northern Victoria were contested by La Trobe University (which wanted to establish a graduate entry medical school in Bendigo, centred on its existing Bendigo campus), and a collaborative bid by the rural clinical schools at Monash and the University of Melbourne (centred on their respective rural campuses in Bendigo and Shepparton).

In northern Victoria the options offered by La Trobe University and the Monash University–University of Melbourne consortium were starkly different in their approach. While the La Trobe University bid was to establish a new graduate entry regional medical school, Monash and the University of Melbourne proposed a model built around their existing rural clinical schools that enhanced rural enrolment and allowed students to spend much longer and continuous periods in rural clinical training. The Monash University–University of Melbourne bid was ultimately successful, so by the end of 2006 the 'educational scramble for Victoria' was over, and the educational landscape was significantly transformed. In parallel with the expansion in medical education, there was a similar if not greater expansion in nursing, allied health and dentistry education programs in Victoria.

Since this expansion has occurred, almost exclusively, in regional rather than metropolitan education programs, it has required the participation of virtually all health services, sizeable general practices and health-related agencies in Victoria. The rapid incorporation of partners, in many cases with very little past involvement or experience in health professions education, has posed some challenges for both governance and effective delivery of large-scale distributed health professions education in Victoria. It has, at the same time, provided an important opportunity to involve almost every health professional in the state in the clinical education of the next generation of health practitioners; by providing support for students in this role, professionals enhance the standard of their own clinical practice. Seen in this way these expanded programs represent not only a significant educational and health workforce intervention but also a very significant strategy for improving health services in Victoria.

By the end of 2006 the medical educational landscape in Victoria was split into distinct regions with NVRMEN covering the northern and central parts of the state.

The NVRMEN model

In opting to build this expansion around existing rural clinical schools rather than to create a new regional medical school, Monash and the University of Melbourne were able to retain their current educational focus on the clinical years while more effectively addressing the health workforce imperatives of their rural clinical school programs. They were also able to redevelop many of their existing facilities, to extend their partner base to include many new small health services, community-based practices and other community health agencies, and to recruit a new cohort of students. They were predominantly from rural areas, with a pre-enrolment commitment to extended placement in northern Victorian rural education sites for over 80 per cent of their clinical training. This new cohort of 60 students – 30 at each university, enrolled under the umbrella of the NVRMEN collaboration – is referred to as the 'Extended Rural Cohort' at both universities.

Collaboration with the University of Melbourne

Both universities saw in their collaboration the opportunity to align their medical education programs across two adjacent rural regions that together constitute a third of the land mass of Victoria. This brought the academic resources of two leading Group of Eight universities to bear on a well-circumscribed rural population of 600,000 people. It also provided the unusual opportunity to tackle, in concert, the health workforce and health service priorities and thereby improve the health status of these communities.

Opening of the Bendigo Regional Clinical School redevelopment 2010: left to right – Georgia von Guttner (University of Melbourne), Peter Disler (Bendigo Health), Dawn DeWitt (University of Melbourne), Jacinta Allan (Victorian Minister for Regional and Rural Development), Geoff Solarsh, and Graham Allardice (Monash University).

The two universities signed a memorandum of agreement which provided for ongoing management by each university of its existing sites, and catered for the placement of University of Melbourne students in prescribed numbers at Monash's Bendigo Regional Clinical School and its affiliated regional hospital. At the outset both universities recognised the special challenges of aligning two different curricula and meeting their separate academic requirements at sites where students from both universities were placed. They also recognised the leverage that could be obtained by working together, as demonstrated by the considerable infrastructural resources secured by this consortium for the NVRMEN initiative in northern Victoria.

Infrastructure development

A total of $25 million dollars of new funding was obtained to develop the physical infrastructure for the NVRMEN initiative. This allowed each university to improve facilities in their respective regional centres. Monash built a new regional clinical school on the Bendigo Health campus and significantly extended our regional clinical school in Mildura. Funding also allowed Monash to establish three rural hubs in the Loddon Mallee region, centred on Kyneton, Castlemaine and Swan Hill. Each hub was provided with dedicated educational facilities and resources to support a distributed model of community-based medical education in multiple general practices and health-related community agencies. Additional funding was obtained for the development of student consulting suites and small educational precincts in each of the participating general practices.

Selection and enrolment

The universities agreed to run a joint process to recruit the first cohort of students in 2007. The shared goal was to recruit as many rural-origin students as possible from the Loddon Mallee and Hume districts in northern Victoria. Failing that, the following recruits were sought, in descending order of priority: rural-origin students from elsewhere in Victoria; rural-origin students from elsewhere in Australia; and, finally, metropolitan students. The usual definition for rural-origin students was used. Information sessions were run at every small rural centre in northern Victoria and publicity campaigns for this new stream of education were launched by both universities through their usual recruitment channels at high schools across Australia. A new Extended Rural Cohort enrolment code was created at the Victorian Tertiary Admissions Centre so that students could pre-select this option in preference to the standard stream at both universities. All students finally selected for the Extended Rural Cohort stream at Monash were expected to sign a contractual agreement that they would be based at regional and rural clinical education sites in northern Victoria in their clinical years.

Pre-clinical education

NVRMEN continues to rely on its Melbourne campuses – the University of Melbourne in Parkville and Monash in Clayton – for the first two years of largely pre-clinical education. This decision allows Extended Rural Cohort students to benefit from the rich resources the central campuses provide in the basic biomedical, social and population sciences, and to enjoy the formative social experience of large campus life. The strong, active presence of the Monash rural health club, Wildfire, on the Clayton campus has provided a vehicle for Extended Rural Cohort student involvement in rural health initiatives during their two-year stay on the metro campus. Short-term rural placements in the early years also provide opportunities for Extended Rural Cohort students to be placed in Bendigo and Mildura and to develop early links with staff and clinical Extended Rural Cohort students based in these schools.

Educational philosophy

Student cohorts on long-term placement in a single circumscribed educational system provide opportunities for learning that are not available in less continuous learning environments. Educational access to the same students over time makes it possible to plan and facilitate sequenced and incremental learning, to have much greater control over educational inputs and to assume greater educational responsibility – with its attendant satisfaction – for distal learning outcomes. However, in NVRMEN, this commitment to educational continuity goes beyond that of the curriculum. Regional systems of care with well-defined primary care systems that have clear, bi-directional referral relationships with more sophisticated, specialised levels of care provide opportunities to understand continuity of care and its effect on the health of both individuals and whole populations. Students in this program move between large regional hospitals, small community hospitals, general practices, community health agencies and households at different points in their three-year clinical training. Our hope is that they will develop well-balanced biomedical, social and population perspectives on the many conditions they encounter, and a good understanding of how health systems at all levels of care make appropriate contributions to their management. Such broad perspectives are particularly important for chronic diseases which represent an ever-increasing proportion of the disease burden in Australia.

Curriculum development

At the inception of NVRMEN, both Monash University and the University of Melbourne already had well-established rural medical education programs in their respective regions and, therefore, considerable pooled experience in customising medical curricula for rural contexts.

Clinical year 1

It had been agreed that students from both universities would do their foundation clinical year in internal medicine, general surgery and their related sub-disciplines together in Bendigo. Since the core curriculum content and hospital-based format were very similar at both universities, it was further agreed that the foundation year would be delivered as a single integrated year-long program for all students, irrespective of their university of origin. In preparation for the first clinical year in 2009, educational teams from Monash and the University of Melbourne, with the assistance of an external consultant, met repeatedly to analyse the two curricula, to map learning objectives and content, and to develop appropriate learning methods that would meet the assessment needs of both universities. This task was complicated by the fact that the two programs had commencement times that were six months apart and that there was a strong likelihood that the University of Melbourne would introduce a totally new curriculum in a few years time. In the end, agreement was reached on a hybrid model that incorporated some of the best elements of both curricula and could be feasibly implemented until clarity about future changes to the University of Melbourne medical course could be provided.

Clinical year 2

The other large curriculum development exercise tackled under the NVRMEN banner was the implementation of a longitudinal community-based model for the disciplines of women's health, children's health, psychiatry and general practice in the second clinical year. Monash and the University of Melbourne briefly considered taking this on as a combined and integrated exercise for all Extended Rural Cohort students at both universities and across both regions. Given the complexity of integrating these four discipline-specific curricula, the number of large and small health services and community agencies that would need to be engaged in each region, and the significant mismatch between curriculum content at the two universities, Monash and the University of Melbourne decided to implement this model separately in their respective regions. At Monash, this exercise was preceded by a protracted community engagement process with rural and regional general practices over a two-year period. The process included an in-depth survey of specialist and general practitioner beliefs about who should teach which parts of the curriculum. Based on the survey, on a detailed mapping of the four component curricula, and on an analysis of individual site capacity for student placements, a final model was determined. It also met our pre-set goals for community-basing, disciplinary integration and year-long educational continuity.

In this year-long model students are expected to cover the children's health, women's health psychiatry and general practice curricula through the course of the year in both regional and rural practice settings. Their time is thus divided equally between semester-long rural and regional rotations which are supervised by generalists and specialists respectively. The detailed mapping of the content of all four curricula and a careful allocation of defined components of this content to rural or regional rotations for generalist or specialist delivery provides year-long continuity and, where appropriate, integration of disciplinary perspectives.

In the rural rotations students are based in a single general practice in one of the rural hubs for 18 weeks, during which they see their own booked patients for two days a week under the supervision of a clinical GP tutor. Another two days are spent linking with multiple community agencies in the same rural primary care system in which their general practices are based and in following selected patients with chronic health conditions through their multiple contacts with other health professionals at different levels in this system. The remaining day of the week is a learning day devoted to tutorials conducted by generalist tutors, and self-directed study.

In the regional rotations students move between three discipline-specific and largely hospital-based blocks in women's health, children's health and psychiatry on four days of the week, and the fifth day is spent in a regional general practice. Discipline-specific tutorials, largely from specialist tutors, are run after 4.00 pm on four days of the week so that they do not interfere with clinical clerkships in the hospital.

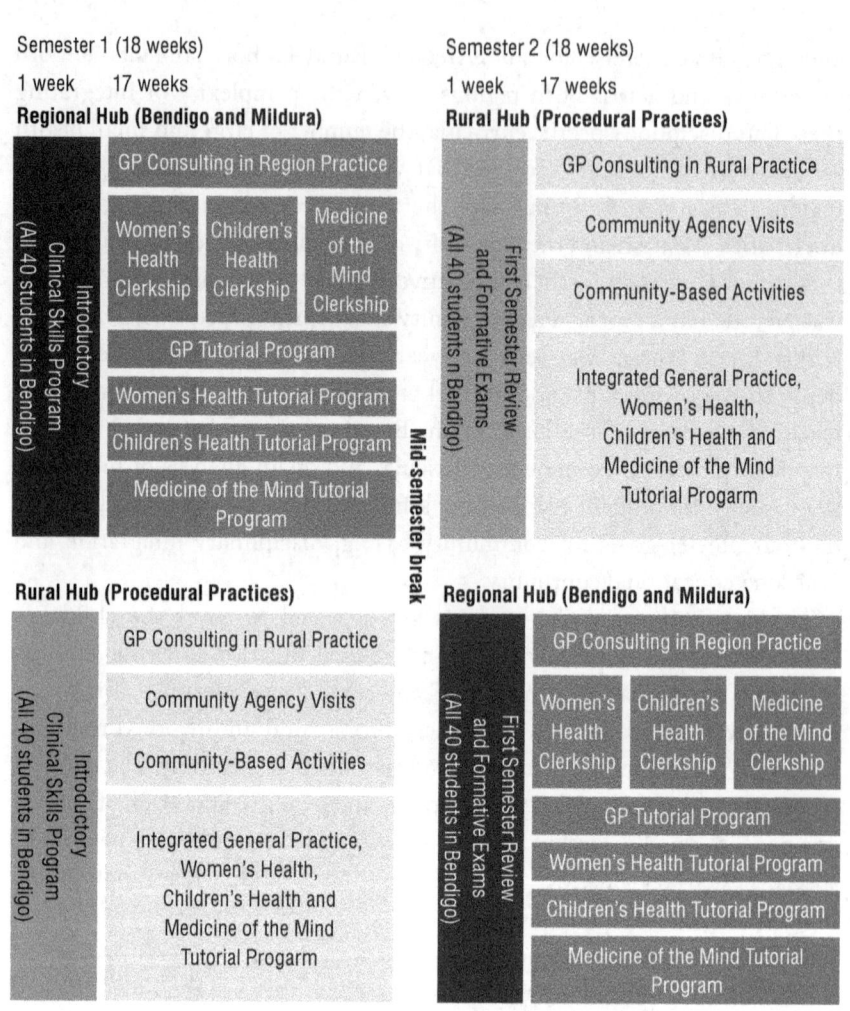

The NVRMEN Year 4 integrated, community-based model launched in 2009.

Clinical year 3

The final year of the Monash medical course comprises a series of hospital-based six-week block rotations that are intended to prepare students for their upcoming internship. There are four core block rotations that include internal medicine, general surgery, aged care and emergency medicine; there is also a Monash selective from a wide range of traditional and non-traditional specialist and generalist options; and, finally, an elective block at any medical school inside or outside Australia.

Monash Extended Rural Cohort students are expected to spend a minimum of two rotations in Bendigo or Mildura. There is anecdotal evidence to suggest that student choices about future career directions and locations are influenced by the exposure they receive in the year before graduation. At a minimum these exposures seem to influence their choices about where to do their internship, which in turn, influences decisions about training programs and their location. Given these observations, and the considerable investment already made in extended rural immersion during the preceding clinical years, it was considered important to base students for some time in the same regional and rural settings in clinical year 3.

It was equally necessary to give our students some exposure to large metropolitan sub-specialist hospitals to round off their clinical training. Not only are there critical perspectives about patient care to be gained, but many Extended Rural Cohort students will spend significant periods of training in these hospitals. Understanding the principles and contribution of sub-specialist services to patient care and the culture of practice in these hospitals is essential for graduates, irrespective of the individual decisions they make about their further medical vocation.

Steps to a regional academic health complex in Bendigo

The Monash Primary Care Clinic

Monash established a primary care clinic in Bendigo in the early 1990s long before the advent of the rural clinical school. This initiative of the Monash Department of General Practice was intended to provide a GP service to disadvantaged communities in Bendigo and to create an exemplar of best practice from which vocational GP training of the highest quality could be conducted. This clinic came to fill a specific niche in Bendigo by providing episodic care for those patients who, for multiple reasons, were not or could not be registered with established general practices. It also provided cover for patients of these other practices when their GPs were away. When the Bendigo Regional Clinical School was established, it took over management of the Primary Care Clinic in 2001.

The Primary Care Clinic has struggled, throughout its existence, to achieve full financial viability. Monash was advised that, unless the Primary Care Clinic significantly increased its patient base and developed service and business models similar to those of other private general practices in Bendigo, the financial issues were unlikely to be reversed. It was also the University's view that the Primary Care Clinic was rightfully a public health asset of the City of Greater Bendigo and that, unless broad-based support could be demonstrated for its continuation, it might need to be closed. In 2007, at much the same time that NVRMEN was established, steps were taken to mobilise a broad-based consortium that would take collective responsibility for further developing the Primary Care Clinic as an ongoing primary health care facility for the people of Bendigo. The consortium was made up of Bendigo Health, Bendigo Community Health Services, Monash University, La Trobe University, Central Victorian General Practice Network, Beyond Medical Education – a GP vocational training provider – and the City of Greater Bendigo. This consortium of seven education and service providers, representing the key players in the primary care space in Bendigo, went on to secure $8.4 million of combined federal GP Super Clinic and state funding that finally enabled the Bendigo Primary Care Centre to be completed in October 2011.

Bendigo Primary Care Centre

Beyond its obvious value as a new purpose-built primary care provider for the people of Bendigo, the Bendigo Primary Care Centre has had a foundational role in building the next phase of health partnerships in the Loddon Mallee region. The shared aspiration for an integrated primary health care service for the City of Greater Bendigo kept the consortium of seven key institutions working together over an intense four-year period, with many ups and downs. It resulted in a protracted and in-depth conversation that has produced a future vision for a city-wide management strategy for chronic non-communicable diseases. It also cemented a set of trusted institutional relationships on which future collaborations could be built.

La Trobe University Rural Health School

La Trobe University has always been an important education provider to the nursing and allied health workforce in Victoria. The La Trobe University response to the expansion of health professions education in Australia has been to establish a new regional dental school in Bendigo and, thereafter, to reconceptualise and expand their nursing and allied health program through the establishment of a rural health school in Bendigo. This school serves as the hub for a distributed health professions education program and student placement strategy that has largely the same geographical footprint, educational philosophy and health workforce goals as the medical education programs run by Monash University and the University of Melbourne under the NVRMEN collaboration. The decision to build part of the La Trobe University Rural Health School adjacent to the Monash regional clinical school and the Bendigo Primary Care Centre has consolidated the health education and research precinct on the Bendigo campus.

Health education and research precinct

This precinct is now home to the Monash Bendigo Regional Clinical School, the coordinating hub for a distributed medical education program in the Loddon Mallee region with links to the adjacent Hume region through the NVRMEN collaboration with the University of Melbourne. It is also home to the La Trobe University Rural Health School, the clinical teaching building for nursing, allied health and dentistry. Finally, it is home to the Bendigo Primary Care Centre, an academic primary care clinic providing comprehensive primary health care to the people of Bendigo. It is a focal point for integrated management of chronic non-communicable diseases in Bendigo and, in time, models of interprofessional education for Monash and La Trobe University students from medical, nursing and allied health backgrounds.

The future influence of this precinct on health professions education, health workforce expansion and health services development in Bendigo and northern Victoria is potentially very large. It provides a concentration of resources and institutional relationships in Bendigo and the region that can now begin to systematically address some of the key health challenges in this region. Established research groups in public health, health services research, health professions education and rural mental health already exist at Monash University and La Trobe University. The next important step will be to build the necessary collaborations between these institutions and research groups, and to develop a shared population platform to support this combined research strategy.

Redevelopment of the Bendigo Hospital

In parallel with these developments there has been an ongoing campaign by Bendigo Health for the redevelopment of its ageing regional hospital. In 2010 the Victorian Government confirmed that $640 million would be set aside for this purpose. It is anticipated that the new hospital will be completed in 2016. With its co-located health education and research precinct, the new regional hospital will constitute one of the largest regional academic health complexes in Australia. Key challenges for the future will be to develop a shared vision for this complex and to understand what distinguishes its mandate from similar academic health complexes in metropolitan centres.

An essential guiding principle in defining this mandate will be to insist that, ultimately, it measurably improves the health status of its defined catchment population. For this to occur, the complex will need to have close links with smaller health services in the region and be committed to working with them to address what are known to be the health priorities for its regional populations. It will also need to rely on its academic partners to develop a future workforce for the region and to assist with the many research activities that underpin an ambitious mandate of this kind.

A regional health and workforce strategy

Health Workforce Australia

Following its announcement of expanded health professions education programs for professional entry students in 2006, the federal government began to prepare for the new demands that this expansion would make on health service and education providers. In 2010, after extensive deliberations and stakeholder consultations, a new statutory body, Health Workforce Australia, was established through a Council of Australian Governments agreement and with a starting budget of $1.6 billion. Its brief was to provide a skilled, flexible and innovative health workforce that meets the needs of the Australian community. Since its inception, Health Workforce Australia has distributed considerable financial resources through the various state governments to meet this mandate. In Victoria, 11 clinical placement networks have been established to provide an accountable governance framework to distribute, manage and evaluate the effectiveness of these new funding streams.

Clinical placement networks

In the Loddon Mallee region, clinical placement networks were recognised early as natural and very valuable extensions to the many strategies and programs that were already in place in this region. They provide a formal organisational framework for multiple health service and education providers to convene at a regional level and to transparently discuss their respective health workforce and training needs and how these might be met using the many new streams of available funding. A critical success factor in these networks is goodwill and trust between their members. The well-established collaborations and relationships already in place in the Loddon Mallee region allowed the clinical placement network to be set up very quickly and to become functional within a very short period of time. While many of the larger health institutions in both Bendigo and Mildura were already linked through existing agreements, it was recognised that similar links with smaller health services and community agencies were less well developed. The clinical placement network provided a well-funded vehicle to bring smaller services into these collaborations and to provide them with a fair share of the resources for their important roles in widely distributed health professions education programs in the region. In addition, the clinical placement network provided a new opportunity to establish a shared vision for health professions education throughout the region and for all stakeholders to engage, on an ongoing basis, around a health workforce strategy for the region. Some specific projects illustrate the broad vision and specific directions that emerged through this process.

Whole of system placements

An important feature of the NVRMEN community-based educational model is the immersion of students for extended periods of time in rural primary health care systems. It is in these systems, tasked with providing comprehensive health care in close proximity to patients' homes, that a special opportunity exists to understand holistic patient-centred care. This is especially true for chronic conditions that require multi-professional inputs at different levels of the health care system. While provision had been made in our previous model for students to spend two of their five days each week exploring these systems, we have struggled to fully demonstrate the link between the patients they see in their GP consulting sessions and the somewhat disconnected visits they make to other local health agencies.

Strategic project funding through the Loddon Mallee Clinical Placement Network has allowed us to reconceptualise this model in collaboration with the La Trobe University Rural Health School. We are currently piloting an alternative model – involving students from medicine, nursing and relevant allied health disciplines – in which students identify patients with chronic conditions in a range of practice environments. They then track the journeys of these patients and the various contacts they make with care providers from multiple disciplines at different levels of the local health care system. These case studies are discussed and developed by multi-professional student groups with a brief to explore the biomedical, social and population perspectives generated by patient journeys. Case studies have the potential to shed light not only on student learning but also on the ways that the health service functions – or does not function – with benefits for both the academy and the service itself. This project is ongoing.

A distributed simulated learning environment

The Loddon Mallee Clinical Placement Network has recently been successful in obtaining over $2 million to develop a distributed simulated learning environment for the region. This project establishes a primary simulation education hub in Bendigo and a secondary hub in Mildura. It significantly supplements the simulation resources held by Monash and La Trobe University on the health education and research precinct in Bendigo and those held by Monash at its regional clinical school in Mildura. A condition of this funding is that La Trobe University and Monash University – at the regional clinical schools in Bendigo and Mildura – provide regular access to these facilities for other health education and health service providers through so-called 'in-reach' and 'out-reach' simulation education programs. The in-reach program makes specific time and space allocations for other institutions to train their learners in these hub facilities, while the outreach program requires simulation education teams from Bendigo and Mildura to visit designated smaller health services on a regular, rostered basis, to service their needs for clinical education using simulation as the main modality.

This project requires Monash University and La Trobe University to conduct a careful educational needs analysis in all smaller centres and to work with local clinical educators to design and implement educational sessions that meet these needs. These are important new responsibilities for regional education providers. The project will improve their understanding of the educational needs of health professional students and practitioners at all stages in their career and pinpoint the opportunities for the use of simulation education. It is also an investment by these providers in the development of a health workforce for the region as a whole. Finally it locks providers into ongoing relationships with every small health service in the Loddon Mallee region.

The future

The 10-year establishment of rural medical education programs for Monash in northern Victoria has seen many phases of growth and development. Programs and perspectives have shifted from institution-specific and discipline-specific to an increasingly complex tapestry of cross-institutional collaborations and new alignments. Health professions education is now the business of all large and small education and health service providers, and related agencies in northern Victoria. It is no longer restricted to professional entry students but also includes health graduates from every profession across the continuum of pre-vocational, vocational and continuing education.

This learning platform straddles large regional hospitals, smaller community hospitals, general practices, community health services, mental health services, maternal and child health services and aged care, providing access through them to the entire patient population in the region. We are now well placed to design, implement and measure the impacts of region-wide health service and health workforce interventions using some or all parts of this platform. Analogous platforms have been established in other regions of Victoria and in other states in Australia. The development of such platforms is, in our view, the next natural step for health workforce and health services research in this region and potentially elsewhere in Australia.

CHAPTER 6

RESEARCH: COMMUNITY RELEVANCE

EMERITUS PROFESSOR JOHN S HUMPHREYS

Research has long been acknowledged as the hallmark that distinguishes universities from many other educational institutions. From research comes the knowledge to understand the complexity of human life and the evidence upon which to formulate appropriate policies and programs designed to bring about improvement in the health and wellbeing of people.

Compared with the more established areas of medical and health research, the field of rural health research is still in its infancy both in Australia and overseas. Consequently, the scope for innovation and new discoveries (from which we are better able to understand the pattern of health and wellbeing in rural and remote areas globally) is enormous. In this regard, the Monash School of Rural Health has played a significant role in generating new knowledge relating to overcoming the rural health workforce shortage, developing innovative rural models of health care and understanding the risk determinants that underpin current rural health disadvantage.

Today, Monash University is one of the leading institutions of research and higher learning in Australia and the world. Within Monash University, the School of Rural Health has pioneered rural Australian health research aimed at bringing about improvements in the health and wellbeing of residents of rural, remote and regional communities, and is now acknowledged as a world leader in this field. Since its inception, too, the research program of the school has assisted to build the research capacity of rural health practitioners and stakeholders.

This chapter outlines the growth of rural health research within the school. Highlights include some of the main outcomes; individuals who have been instrumental in the international recognition of the research program;

keys to success; and the challenges which the school will have to confront in the future.

Research development in the School of Rural Health

The need for a dedicated rural health research program emanates from the activities of key stakeholder groups such as the Rural Doctors Association of Australia, the New South Wales Rural Doctors Network, the Association of Australian Rural Nurses and the Council of Remote Area Nurses during the 1980s and early 1990s.[1] These groups advocated strongly for the need to address outstanding rural health issues that had been highlighted as early as 1976 in the Hospitals and Health Commission report. It specifically featured the following: the difficulties faced by many country people in obtaining adequate health care; the shortage of doctors, dentists and other health personnel; difficulties in maintaining health facilities in many communities; and the appalling plight of Aboriginal health.[2] The debate highlighted not only the comparative neglect of rural health by governments, but also the lack of understanding of these problems and why residents of rural and remote areas were characterised by a significantly poorer health status than that of their metropolitan counterparts.

The development of rural health research in the School of Rural Health was oriented towards redressing this knowledge gap and falls broadly into three phases, each of which is discussed below.

1992–2002: Establishing the Centre for Rural Health

During this period, most research activity was linked with project funding from the Commonwealth and Victorian Departments of Health and fell within four broad areas: rural health as a specific discipline; collaborative clinical research; rural health workforce recruitment and retention; and development of models of health service delivery in rural communities. Research highlights included the National Rural General Practice Study and Sustainable Models of Rural and Remote General Practice Services. Much of this research activity was closely related to the lead role assumed in government consultancies and national reviews of general practice. Research leaders at Monash during this period included Roger Strasser, Jo Wainer, Elaine Duffy, Claire Rickard, Gil Soo-Han and Peter O'Meara.

In addition to the specific research undertaken by individual staff, the Centre for Rural Health played a vitally important role in research capacity building and the dissemination of key resources for rural health research. In the early 1990s, national competitive funding was awarded to the Centre for Rural Health to lead in developing a National Rural Health Unit – later renamed the Australian Rural Health Research Institute. This unit was a collaboration between Monash University, Menzies School of Health Research Northern Territory, Charles Sturt University, the University of Western Australia and the University of South Australia, and was mandated to assume a clearing house role for rural health research, training, education and data.

Prior to the 'take-off' of electronic literature searches, the Centre for Rural Health also maintained a leading role in supporting and servicing the information and research needs of rural community practitioners through Literature Information Service for Australian Rural and Remote Health and the Rural Health Research Register which increased the dissemination of, and access to, publications relevant to rural health. This period also saw the development of Echidna: Health Service Profiles for Victorian Rural Regions – an electronic database of information relating to localities, health services, demographics and other health-related indicators for communities across rural Victoria.

During its early years, research staff from the Centre for Rural Health were well represented at national conferences and symposia in the dissemination of research project findings; the apogee was perhaps the centre's representation at the invitation-only Regional Australia Summit at Parliament House Canberra, auspiced by the Deputy Prime Minister and the Department of Transport and Regional Services.

2002–2007: Research 'take-off' phase

In 2002, following a faculty restructure, the Centre for Rural Health became the School of Rural Health and set up a dedicated research office in Bendigo, which I led as newly appointed Professor of Rural Health Research. This development, together with the acquisition of funding to establish a Centre for Multi-Disciplinary Studies in Rural Health in Gippsland under the leadership of Elaine Duffy, enabled the consolidation of research activity around two nodes – Moe-Traralgon in Gippsland and Bendigo in the Loddon Mallee region – and provided a major impetus for research 'take-off'. These developments paralleled funding to establish a rural clinical school network from East Gippsland to Mildura. In 2006, further funding was received to incorporate the Centre for Multi-Disciplinary Studies in Rural Health into a fully fledged university department of rural health. It was renamed MUDRIH (Monash University Department of Rural and Indigenous Health) under the directorship of Mark Oakley Browne. Under his leadership, and guided by the School of Rural Health research strategy, the rural health research platform has been significantly strengthened in Gippsland.

Research activity gained momentum, with a dramatic increase in both the publication of peer-reviewed journal articles and the acquisition of nationally competitive grants from funding bodies such as the Australian Research Council, National Health and Medical Research Council (NHMRC), and Australian Primary Health Care Research Institute. During this period the School of Rural Health was accorded a change of research status within the faculty from 'an area targeted for development' to that of 'a recognised area of strength competitive with the best domestic equivalents'. The Viable Models of Rural Practice study, undertaken in conjunction with the Rural Doctors Association of Australia, exemplified the important workforce research being undertaken within the school.

During this phase, the successful development of a postgraduate research program in Traralgon by Gil Soo-Han led to the graduation of the school's first PhD candidates, thereby increasing rural health research capacity in the region. During this time too, the school took pride in the appointment of two of its leading researchers to senior academic posts. Claire Rickard went to Tasmania and subsequently Queensland, and Gil Soo-Han to Monash Malaysia and subsequently Clayton.

At the same time, the appointment of a new professoriate in Bendigo – Professors Fiona Judd, Gordon Whyte and Peter Disler – contributed immensely to the development of a strong research culture in the region. It had strong links between researchers from the school and the newly established Centre for Rural Mental Health, a joint activity of Bendigo Health and Monash, based on the Bendigo Hospital campus and led by Professor Fiona Judd. The research team also welcomed its first epidemiologist, Dr Geetha Ranmuthagala, from the National Centre for Epidemiology and Population Health at the Australian National University.

So significant was the school's education, training and research program that, in 2005, 40 leading medical workforce academics, policy makers and educators from the UK, Canada and USA were hosted in Bendigo at the invitation of the International Medical Workforce Collaborative. In addition, research staff from the school were instrumental in working closely with the Committee of Deans of Australian Medical Schools to set up the national Medical Students Outcomes Database and longitudinal tracking study, one of the recommendations emanating from the review of the Australian Government Rural Undergraduate Support and Coordination program.

Conference, Bendigo 2005: International medical workforce academics, policy makers and educators from the UK, Canada and USA.

2007–2012: National and international pre-eminence

The establishment of the graduate entry Gippsland Medical School and the Northern Victoria Rural Medical Education Network in 2007 were important developments that boosted research within the school. Newly appointed research leaders at the Gippsland Medical School, including Elmer Villanueva and Debra Nestel, helped consolidate the research status of the School of Rural Health in Gippsland. During this period the research reputation of the school grew to one of national and international pre-eminence. This reputation was endorsed by the Research Quality Framework assessment undertaken by the Australian Government in 2008, an evaluation process which morphed into the current Excellence of Research in Australia evaluation process.

Consistent with the University's mandate of excellence in research, this phase also saw the consolidation of school-wide research culture – exemplified in the regular research newsletters and by a highly successful journal club that brings research staff together monthly – with a greater orientation for evidence-based research to inform policy and practice. The school's strong presence in the policy arena was typified by invited presentations to parliamentarians in Canberra in 2010 and 2011 in relation to the rural medical workforce crisis, and the launch in Parliament House Canberra of the Australian Primary Health Care Research Institute-funded Workforce Retention study by the Minister for Rural Remote and Aboriginal Affairs, Warren Snowden.

Nationally acclaimed research achievements included the work of Marlene Drysdale who led both the Footprints Forwards: Better Strategies for the Recruitment, Retention and Support of Indigenous Students Project and the Rural Chronic Disease Initiative. The jewel in the crown was the award, in late 2010, of $3 million research funding to lead the Centre of Research Excellence in Rural and Remote Primary Health Care – a collaboration of staff from the School of Rural Health, the Flinders and Charles Darwin Universities Centre for Remote Health in Alice Springs, and the University of Sydney Department of Rural Health in Broken Hill.[3] The Centre of Research Excellence was launched on 20 September 2011 in Parliament House Canberra by the Minister for Mental Health and Ageing, Mark Butler.

Launch of the Centre of Research Excellence 2011: John Humphreys (left) and the Minister for Mental Health and Ageing, Mark Butler (right).

During this phase, significant activity focused on building research capacity. Workshop support provided by staff from the Faculty of Medicine, Nursing and Health Sciences Research Office, and the promotion of opportunities for postgraduate research, paid off. Several early career researchers had increased success in obtaining research grants and the award of two International Travelling Research Fellowships. During this time, the appointment of new researchers also helped to increase the critical mass of research active staff. Research from the school established a greater international presence with research staff invited to present their findings at major national and international conferences in Scotland, Sweden, Germany and Canada.

In short, after 20 years in the making, it is clear that research within the School of Rural Health has come of age.

Significant research achievements

Research within the school has covered a very broad spectrum of issues, including studies investigating specific topics such as rural pharmacy; urgent care; telemedicine; gender issues; mental health; health service complaints; treatment and care of people with developmental disability in rural and remote communities; rural medical education; clinical studies relating to intravenous devices; stroke and osteoporosis; and numerous health policy and program evaluations.

Rural health workforce research

Researchers from the school have been actively engaged in all aspects of the rural health workforce, particularly through investigations on two key issues:

- What aspects of medical and health education and training increase the likelihood of graduates taking up rural practice, thereby increasing the rural health workforce supply?

- What aspects of recruitment and retention require specific policy intervention in order to ensure an adequate rural health workforce?

Several notable national studies were undertaken on rural medical education and training, factors influencing the intention of medical students to practise in rural Australia, recruitment and retention issues, international medical graduates, the roles and functions of health practitioners, and gender issues. Of particular note is the research undertaken by Dr Matthew McGrail in developing an improved 'index of access' to guide workforce planning in rural and remote areas.[4] This innovative research has already received international acclaim.

In addition, staff have played a leading role in the development and conduct of the landmark Medical Student Outcomes Data and Longitudinal Tracking Study which is currently auspiced by the Medical Deans Australia and New Zealand and engages all Australian and New Zealand medical schools.[5] This project has become a critical part of the national agenda to provide evidence for assessing which aspects of medical education and training are most influential in persuading people to take up rural practice – it is being watched with interest by international medical educators. In addition, Marlene Drysdale has led national research investigating opportunities for, and barriers to, Aboriginal student entry to medical education, with a view to developing better approaches that progress recruitment, retention and support for Aboriginal students in medicine.

The school was also a joint partner in a $2 million, five-year collaborative NHMRC grant with the University of Melbourne to undertake the Medicine in Australia: Balancing Employment and Life national longitudinal study of work–life balance for doctors.[6] In 2011 this study received a further five years of funding from the NHMRC as a Centre for Research Excellence in Medical Workforce Dynamics. The research aims to improve the understanding of the determinants of decisions made by doctors on how many hours to work, where to work in terms of sector, geographic location and specialty, when to stop work temporarily or permanently, and productivity. These decisions are, in turn, a key influence on access to health care by the population, health care costs, and ultimately population health.

As a result of this workforce research, School of Rural Health researchers have played a key role in advising government on measures to improve rural health workforce recruitment and retention. Staff have contributed to several key Commonwealth Government workforce program committees that provide advice for national workforce policy development and program implementation, and their expertise has been used by the Australian Government both to undertake program evaluation and to facilitate several national workshops. One notable workshop was the Regional Australia Summit (convened by the Deputy Prime Minister) which was so instrumental in influencing the direction of government measures announced in the landmark 2000–2001 budget that delivered more than $500 million for rural health.[7]

Rural health services research

The demise of health care services in many rural and remote communities through health service rationalisation and centralisation has left many small communities without access to adequate health care despite their great need for it.[8] Over two decades, researchers from the school have pioneered research into alternative, sustainable, innovative models of service delivery for residents of small rural and remote communities.

The longitudinal Elmore Primary Health Service study examined primary health care in a small rural community. The research team in 2008: left to right – Lisa Lavey, Karly Smith, Rachel Tham, Dr Adel Asaid, Judith Jones, Leigh Kinsman, Kathy Tuohey.

Building on several studies undertaken in small communities, the most comprehensive systematic synthesis and typology of rural health service models was published. This research has formed the basis for health service research throughout Australia and helped to set the research agenda about the requirements for sustainable rural health services. Moreover, research staff undertook the Viable Models project – one of the most comprehensive and detailed Australian investigations ever made into the economic, professional and organisation aspects underpinning the viability of rural and remote practice. More recently, in conjunction with researchers from Flinders University in Alice Springs and the Australian National University in Canberra, a comprehensive systematic review of sustainable models of primary care for small rural and remote communities was undertaken to inform policy makers about how best to deliver comprehensive primary health care to areas that currently experience significant problems accessing such services.[9]

Rural Australians are also disadvantaged by lack of access to comprehensive coordinated health care services. At times of emergency in particular, patients are required to undertake extensive travel to access care only available in distant regional centres, often at great personal cost. It is critically important to ensure efficient and effective pathways of care within the health system as the basis for smooth transition between primary and secondary emergency treatment, and subsequent rehabilitative care. Leigh Kinsman's innovative research on clinical pathways and the provision of timely and appropriate emergency care in regional centres has been widely received and utilised nationally and internationally.[10]

Rural health risk determinants research

The explosion of chronic diseases – such as Type 2 diabetes, asthma, heart disease, lung disease, stroke, hypertension, osteoporosis, certain cancers, depression associated with chronic disease, and disabilities caused by preventable injuries – is one of the most pressing problems confronting health services throughout Australia. Chronic diseases present huge costs to the health system, significantly reduce individual quality of life, and reduce economic participation and productivity.

Rural and remote Australians experience higher rates of chronic illness and injury than metropolitan counterparts, with consequent higher morbidity and mortality. The need for effective health promotion, ill-health prevention and early intervention programs for residents of small rural and remote communities, many of which are among Australia's most educationally and socioeconomically disadvantaged groups, is a major challenge for governments, health authorities and communities alike. Research led by Marlene Drysdale and other School of Rural Health researchers has provided the most significant platform for people in small rural communities who want to try new ways to make a difference to chronic disease at a local level.

Investigation of national priority diseases requires complex and proven methodologies in order to accurately identify their incidence, prevalence and aetiology as the basis for policy response. Significant research has been undertaken by Oakley Browne, Ranmuthugala, Villanueva, Ristevski and Mayberry, particularly in the areas of mental health, rural community epidemiological and population cohort studies, and evidence-based planning. Rickard and McGrail have also taken a lead role in examining the efficacy of interventions designed to bring about improved practice in rural health services.

Landmark research projects

Many landmark research projects have been undertaken by research staff. The studies described below all had a significant impact on national rural health policies and programs, and exemplify the importance of research in providing the evidence base upon which to formulate polices designed to overcome problems or assist in improving the health outcomes of rural and remote Australians.

National Rural General Practice study

The purpose of this study was to examine factors influencing the decisions of general practitioners in relation to undertaking general practice. Its specific objectives were to describe the nature of rural and remote area general practice, to investigate rural doctor experience and perceptions of recent initiatives aimed at improving recruitment, training and retention of rural doctors, and to explore the attitudes of rural doctors to changing rural health services.[11]

Viable Models project

Funded by a $2 million Commonwealth Government grant, Monash University researchers collaborated with the Rural Doctors Association to undertake the most detailed study of the determinants of viability of rural and remote practice in Australia. This project undertook a detailed analysis of the complexity and costs of general practice in different rural and remote environments. The research provided the most comprehensive empirical evidence differentiating rural from urban general practice in Australia, and set the benchmarks for practice viability in rural and remote locations. The final report was launched by Minister for Health, Tony Abbot, in November 2003 and the study had a significant impact on government policy, rural doctors and their communities.[12]

Elmore Primary Health Service project

The problem of ensuring sustainable, equitable and quality primary health care services for rural and remote communities is an international issue. The longitudinal Elmore Primary Health Service study – funded by Australian Rotary Health and the Australian Government Department of Health and Ageing – examines the performance, sustainability and impact of a comprehensive primary health care service in a small rural community. The evaluation framework developed has been widely adopted as the basis for informing future rural health service policies.[13]

Footprints Forwards: Better Strategies for the Recruitment, Retention and Support of Indigenous Medical Students

This project investigated opportunities for, and barriers to, Indigenous student entry to medical education with a view to designing suitable resources for use in secondary schools. The three key objectives were to:

- examine existing information relating to Indigenous recruitment and support strategies of Australian Medical Schools
- identify reasons for low Indigenous recruitment, enrolment and completion in medical schools and
- review existing promotional materials, and develop and pilot an interactive multimedia product designed to facilitate flexible and sustainable models of recruitment.

The team produced a promotional DVD titled *You Can Do It!*, and undertook widespread dissemination with key stakeholders to develop approaches to achieve better recruitment, retention and support for Indigenous students in medicine.

Rural Chronic Disease Initiative – Building Healthy Communities Resource Kit

The Rural Chronic Disease Initiative was funded by the Australian Government Department of Health and Ageing to improve what people know about chronic disease, to encourage community members to adopt a healthier lifestyle, and provide better ways to help people with chronic disease. Monash University School of Rural Health researched small rural and remote communities throughout Australia as the basis for developing and distributing high quality information on chronic disease and injury, and supporting and developing skills and leadership in people in small rural communities. This research resulted in a major publication, *Building Healthy Communities – A Guide for Community Projects*, that has become a critically important training resource to guide people in small rural communities who want to try new ways to make a difference to chronic disease at a local level.[14]

Centre of Research Excellence in Rural and Remote Primary Health Care (CRE)

This centre is a collaboration between Monash University School of Rural Health, the Flinders University and Charles Darwin University Centre for Remote Health in Alice Springs, and the University of Sydney Department of Rural Health in Broken Hill.[15] The centre aims to develop:

- a better understanding of health behaviour relating to primary health care service use in rural and remote Australia
- better measures of access to guide resource allocation relating to primary health care in small rural and remote communities
- a comprehensive framework for evaluating the impact of rural and remote primary health care services on access and equity of health outcomes
- evidence-based models of sustainable primary health care for different rural and remote contexts.

Indicators of success

Over the 20-year period, research staff have achieved widespread success in gaining competitive research funding and in publishing extensively in peer-reviewed journals (see table: Research performance indicators 1992-2012). Publications have increased significantly over the 20-year period, accompanied by an increase in articles published in high-impact rural health journals. The increasing importance and impact of the contribution of rural health publications and expertise is seen in journal citations, keynote presentations at national and international conferences, invited addresses, reviewer status and membership of government rural health advisory committees. In terms of research funding, most grants in the early years of the Centre of Rural Health fell into Category 2, Other Public Sector Research Income, and emanated mostly from federal and state government sources. Most recently, an increased proportion of research funding has come from nationally competitive granting bodies such as the National Health and Medical Research Council, Australian Research Council and other national competitive grants such as the Australian Primary Health Care Research Institute and Rotary Health. The school is now leading one Centre of Research Excellence and is a joint partner with another. Compared with equivalent rural health research organisations – such as university departments of rural health – Monash University School of Rural Health now rates highly on all research indicators.

Research performance indicators 1992–2012

Year	Number of peer-reviewed publications	Competitive research funding
1992	9[a]	na
1997	32[b]	na
2002	20[c]	$608,607[c]
2007	51[d]	$2,137,000[e]
2012	93[f]	$4,635,300[e]

a 1993/94 Annual Report
b 1997/98 Centre for Rural Health Year in Review
c 2002 Monash University School of Rural Health Year in Review
d 2007 Monash University School of Rural Health Report to Department of Education Science and Training
e Based on Office of Research Records 2007 and 2012
f 2012 Monash University School of Rural Health Report to Department of Industry, Innovation, Science, Research and Tertiary Education.

Importantly too, research undertaken by the school has had a significant impact on rural health policy development. This strong linkage and exchange between rural health researchers and policy decision makers is the result of close collaborations with, and involvement of, key rural health policy makers in reference groups. Such groups have been established to help guide major research projects, and are an important catalyst for ensuring research uptake so that policy and practice are evidence-based. Rural health researchers have also engaged actively in knowledge translation through:

- ensuring research findings are published in a broad range of public outlets – such as in summaries and reports specifically targeting consumer, practitioner and policy audiences – as well as peer-reviewed academic publications
- public research presentations, professional workshops, and community consultation and feedback
- membership and significant involvement in several key government advisory and reference groups
- strong collaborations with health service providers and peak organisations
- media broadcasts
- program monitoring and evaluation research.

The strong research culture and activity that has been developed within the school has had a significant impact on rural health research capacity building. With the advent of postgraduate education in the school, higher degree research students continue to assume an increasingly important role in the school's research program. Moreover, research staff have played a key role in assisting other rural health groups to gain research funding through critical evaluation of grants, mentoring, grant reviews, presentations about research quality, membership of external research funding bodies, and through submissions to national bodies – Australian Rural Health Education Network, NHMRC – for more strategic rural health research funding. The school has 'grown' and 'exported' research leaders who made valuable contributions to its research program, with early career researchers being promoted to senior academic positions – Dr Leigh Kinsman and Dr Gil Soo-Han to associate professorships, and Dr Claire Rickard and Dr Elaine Duffy to professorships at other Australian universities.

Factors contributing to research success

With rural health research in general still in its infancy in many universities, it is timely to reflect on the factors which have contributed to its success within Monash University. These include vision and leadership, faculty and school support, strong stakeholder relationships, a strategic approach, international exposure, mentoring, capacity building and the fostering of a research culture in the School of Rural Health.

Vision and leadership

Undoubtedly the early vision of Roger Strasser, in pioneering the establishment of the Centre of Rural Health in Moe, recognised the need for a strong research presence to parallel government activity designed to address outstanding rural health workforce problems. Roger's decision, strongly supported by then dean of the faculty, Professor Nick Saunders, to appoint Australia's first dedicated Professor of Rural Health Research ensured that the school was characterised by strong research leadership. Through the strategic vision of its early leaders, the school has played a lead role in identifying priority research issues and themes for rural and remote Australia. Many of them have been adopted as the basis for rural health research programs elsewhere in the country.

Faculty and school support

Instrumental in facilitating research success was the strong support from the faculty deans (Professors Porter, Saunders, Byrne, Wesselingh, and Mitchell), deputy deans of research (Professors Michael Berndt, Ian Smith, and Ross Coppel), and heads of school (Professors Roger Strasser, Elaine Duffy, Geoff Solarsh, Gordon Whyte and Judi Walker). Under the school headship of Geoff Solarsh and Gordon Whyte and, more recently, its current head, Judi Walker, research activity received further endorsement. A decision was made to build up research nodes, with sufficient critical mass through geographic consolidation of activity, to foster early career researchers and develop a more viable postgraduate program.

Much of the research success is also attributable to the excellent support provided by the Office of Research staff. In particular, the school's research program owes much to the first-class administrative support provided by the manager of the Office of Research in Bendigo, Lisa Lavey. Testimony to the exemplary role she played were the recognition awards presented to her: the Monash University Vice-Chancellors Award for exceptional performance, and the special individual recognition award for her role as a Research Office Professional from the Australian Institute of Office Professionals Provincial Victorian Office. Lisa's role has been assisted immensely by the strong support she received from Sandra Paschkow and Cathy Ward in Bendigo, while Janelle McGrail provided excellent support in the Gippsland region.

Strong research stakeholder relationships

Central to the strong, successful policy orientation and relevance of much of the research within the school have been the extensive, long-standing and close collaborations with a wide range of rural stakeholders. The school has an established track record of working closely with state and federal governments, universities, a broad range of health service providers, professional organisations and community stakeholder groups, rural workforce agencies, and university departments of rural health. The development of the regional clinical schools provided the opportunity to further establish close research links with clinicians, regional service providers, divisions of general practice and rural communities at local and regional levels. Additionally, the school works closely with researchers from other departments within the faculty, including nursing, primary health care, epidemiology and preventive medicine. Without the support and involvement of these stakeholders, the research undertaken by the school would not have been adopted in the policy and practice arenas to the extent that it has.

Strategic approach to priority research issues

Building on its comparative advantage of geographical locations stretching from Mildura to East Gippsland, staff within the school undertook research on key rural health issues impacting locally, nationally and internationally. The school developed a research strategy targeting the priority goals promoted by the Australian Government, and undertaking evidence-based research to inform government policy. As has been outlined above, major research themes included:

- rural health workforce, including rural medical education and training, factors influencing the intention of medical students to practise in rural Australia, recruitment and retention issues, international medical graduates, the roles and functions of health practitioners, and gender issues
- the development of sustainable models of service delivery in rural and remote areas of Australia
- epidemiological studies designed to better understand the distribution of priority health conditions and the specific effect of health service interventions on health outcomes.

Over the years, strategic planning meetings for research were held regularly at the following places: Phillip Island in 2000; Clayton in 2004; Moe in 2006; Traralgon in 2001 and 2002; and Bendigo in 2005, 2007, 2009, and 2011.

National and international visitors

Since its founding, the school has welcomed some of the world's leading figures in rural and remote health, and their presentations and presence have assisted in fostering a strong research culture. Visitors have included Professors Raymond Pong and Roger Pitblado from the Centre for Remote and Northern Health Research, Laurentian University Ontario Canada; Professor Ivar Aaraas, National Centre of Rural Medicine, University of Tromso; Professor John Wakerman, the Flinders University and Charles Darwin University Centre for Remote Health, Alice Springs; Associate Professor Lisa Bourke, University of Melbourne Department of Rural Health; Professor Jane Farmer, University of Aberdeen; Associate Professor Mike Jones, Macquarie University; Professor

David Lyle and Associate Professor David Perkins, University of Sydney Department of Rural Health; Professors Ian Smith, Michael Berndt, Robin Bell, and Ross Coppell, Monash University; Professor Stephen Campbell, University of Manchester; Professor Joachim Kugler, University of Dresden; Professor Rod Hooker, University of Texas; Professor Gary Hart, University of Washington; Professor Jim Rourke, University of Western Ontario; Dr John Wynn Jones, Institute of Rural Health, Wales; Professor Ruth Endacott, University of Plymouth, England; Professor Ian Couper, University of Witswatersrand, Johannesburg; and Dr John Wootton, Ontario, Canada.

Research mentoring and capacity building

A significant advance in 2001 was the introduction of a full-time postgraduate research program to complement the existing masters and graduate diploma programs in rural health. The school's first two PhD students graduated in 2005, and there is now a robust program for training higher degree research students. A number of other specific measures to increase research skills and productivity were also undertaken, including a week-long Writeway workshop designed to provide inexperienced researchers with the opportunity to participate in a group activity. The aim was to maximise the acceptance of publications by peer-reviewed journals, and foster relationships with research mentors.

Research culture

Developing a strong research culture does not happen overnight, but rather reflects the combination of a commitment to enquiry and new knowledge, support for early career researchers, success in grants and publications and, above all, a clear strategic focus to guide activity. The School of Rural Health has been successful in integrating research into all aspects of its mandate; its success is reflected in the large number of invitations to participate in both national and international conferences and workshops.

Future challenges

The current research environment is highly competitive and the emphasis on strong national and international collaborations will require the School of Rural Health to continue to broaden its outlook and process of engagement. In order to maintain leadership in rural health research, the school will need to build on the factors that have led to its present success and to address some new challenges. Aside from the inherent complexity of many issues that rural health researchers are required to address, new challenges include the following needs: to build stronger research relationships across all nodes of the school; to respond to the requirements of governments and policy makers rapidly; to overcome the 'metro-centric corporatist' paradigm by which rural health research is being governed; to develop a better pipeline into research for persons from health science backgrounds; and to strengthen research methodologies that are appropriate for investigating rural health issues; and to refine the process by which research findings are disseminated and adopted in the policy arena.

Research consolidation

One of the biggest problems confronting rural health researchers is their relative isolation in nodes that lack critical mass and research expertise in areas such as bio-statistics, epidemiology and health economics. The key to overcoming such isolation is consolidation, something which can be achieved through developing strong relationships between the individual sites and the efficient use of IT to support research. Access to a robust and reliable IT system is crucial since it has the ability to transcend distance through instant access to library resources, rapid movement of data, and both visual and aural communication. Videoconferencing now enables access over wide areas to seminars, workshops, journal clubs, and participation in all manner of reference groups and meetings relevant to the research.

Knowledge transfer

Ensuring relevance to all stakeholders, but particularly to governments, is of increasing importance in research. It requires a sound understanding of government, health service, practitioner and consumer needs, and a well-developed strategy for disseminating research evidence and new knowledge. The ongoing involvement of rural health researchers on government advisory committees and health organisation boards is critical in this regard, as is the participation of bureaucrats, service providers and consumers in formulating and conducting the research.

Research governance

Increasing demands of reporting on research outcomes and the growth of the corporatist paradigm in universities has fostered a 'one-coat-fits-all' approach to research. Such an approach works against the flexibility required by rural health researchers who need to adapt their investigations and methodologies to the context in which they are working. An inflexible system alienates key stakeholders because it fails to work with them as equal partners and unnecessarily complicates the way in which research is conducted at the local level.

Research capacity

Most university pipelines into research are very traditional and fail to recognise that many health practitioners interested in undertaking research in conjunction with their practice do not easily fulfil the pre-requisites for postgraduate research. Nor does their heavy workload enable them to leave the workforce and take on research full-time. What is required is the development of innovative pathways which facilitate entry into research without devaluing its standards and rigour.

Research methodology and knowledge translation

Rural health issues are 'wicked problems'.[16] As such, adherence to traditional scientific methods, such as randomised control trials, are often not appropriate or cannot be used, thereby requiring the development of alternative robust methodologies. The effective use of mixed methods, both quantitative and qualitative, in the best rural health studies, exemplifies the importance of establishing timely, appropriate relationships with all persons involved with, and affected by, the research being undertaken. The process is time-consuming and demands great expertise, understanding and sensitivity on the part of the researcher; nowhere is this more important than in working with Aboriginal Australians. Moreover, the research findings must be shared and disseminated in diverse ways for different audiences.

A critical role in the future

Over its first 20 years, research activity at the School of Rural Health has matured into a program that has national and international significance. Its current high status reflects the enormous work undertaken by everyone associated with research in the school. The strategic research undertaken by the researchers from the school has had a very significant impact on the development of new knowledge as well as on national policies and programs designed to address rural health problems of workforce shortage, health service provision and poor health status that characterise rural and remote Australia. This high impact and take-up of research from the school reflects the applied nature of the investigations and the close engagement and collaboration the school maintains with rural hospitals, rural workforce agencies, divisions of general practice, rural doctors associations, Commonwealth and state governments, and numerous professional and community organisations. Guided by the Monash University research strategy imperatives of excellence, relevance and impact, there is no doubt that the research program within the school will continue to play a critical role over the next 20 years.

Endnotes

1. Chater, A. 1993. 'The role of the National Rural Health Alliance'. *Australian Journal of Rural Health* 1 (2): 5–12.
2. Hospitals and Health Services Commission. 1976. 'Rural health in Australia: A report'. Canberra: Australian Government Publishing Service.
3. See the centre's website: http://www.crerrphc.org.au.
4. McGrail, M; Humphreys, J. 2009. 'A new index of access to primary care services in rural areas'. *Australian and New Zealand Journal of Public Health* 33 (5): 418–423.
5. See the medical deans' website: http://www.medicaldeans.org.au/projects-activities/msod.
6. See the Medicine in Australia: Balancing Employment and Life website: https://mabel.org.au/.
7. Department of Infrastructure and Transport. 2008. 'The Regional Australia Summit'[Internet]. Australian Government. Accessed July 2012. Available from: http://www.infrastructure.gov.au/department/annual_report/1999_2000/RegionalAustraliaSummit.aspx.
8. Humphreys, J; Dixon, J. 2004. 'Access and equity in Australian rural health services'. In *Accessing Health Care: Responding to Diversity*, edited by Healy, J.; & McKee, M. Oxford: Oxford University Press: 89–107.
9. Wakerman, J; Humphreys, J; Wells, R; Kuipers, P; Entwistle, P; Jones, J. 2006. 'A systematic review of primary health care delivery models in rural and remote Australia 1993-2006'. Canberra: Australian Primary Health Care Research Institute. Available from http://aphcri.anu.edu.au/research-program/aphcri-network-research-completed/stream-four-translating-evidence-policy/systematic-review-primary.
10. Kinsman, L; Champion, R; Lee, G; Martin, M; Masman, K; May, E; Mills, T; Taylor, M; Thomas, P; Williams, R; Zalstein, S. 2008. 'Assessing the impact of streaming in a regional emergency department'. *Emergency Medicine Australasia* 20: 221–222.
    Rotter, T; Kinsman, L; Kugler, J; Gothe, H; James, E; Snow, P; Willis, J; Machotta, A. 2010. 'Clinical pathways: Effects on professional practice, patient outcomes, length of stay and hospital costs (systematic review)'. Cochrane Database of Systematic Reviews 3:CD006632.
11. School of Rural Health, Office of Research. 2008. 'National Rural General Practice Study (NRGPS) – Executive Summary & Final Report'. [Internet]. Monash University. Accessed June 2012. Available from: http://www.med.monash.edu.au/srh/research/nrgps/.

12   Viable Models Management Committee. 2003. 'Viable models of rural and remote practice: Stage 1 and stage 2 reports'. [Internet]. Rural Doctors Association of Australia. Accessed June 2012. Available from: http://www.rdaa.com.au/Uploads/Documents/Stage%201%20and%20Stage%202%20Reports_20110224092844.pdf.

13   Tham, R; Humphreys, J; Kinsman, L; Buykx, P; Asaid, A; Tuohey, K; Riley, K. 2010. 'Evaluating the impact of sustainable comprehensive primary health care on rural health'. *Australian Journal of Rural Health* 18 (4): 166–172.

14   Department of Health and Ageing. 2004. 'Building Healthy Communities'. [Internet]. Australian Government. Accessed August 2012. Available from: http://www.health.gov.au/internet/main/publishing.nsf/Content/ruralhealth-pubs-BHC.htm.

15   See the Centre of Research Excellence in Rural and Remote Primary Health Care web site: http://www.crerrphc.org.au.

16   Humphreys, J; Kuipers, P; Wakerman, J; Wells, R; Jones, J; Kinsman, L. 2009. 'How far can systematic reviews inform the policy development for "wicked" rural health service problems?'. *Australian Health Review* 33 (4): 592–600.

CHAPTER 7

ABORIGINAL HEALTH: LEADING THE WAY

ADJUNCT PROFESSOR MARLENE DRYSDALE

Prior to 2002 Monash University had not committed to including Aboriginal and Torres Strait Islander health in the medical, nursing and health sciences curricula. However, there were some committed staff members and unit coordinators who included information and lectures about Aboriginal health where possible. Evidence showed, and still does, that Aboriginal people have the worst health status of any group in Australia, and there was a call at the national level to do something about the situation.

In 2002 Dr Janice Chesters and Dr John Togno, two passionate advocates of Aboriginal health, approached me to ask if I would be interested in setting up the Indigenous Health Unit at the School of Rural Health under the leadership of Professor Roger Strasser. After several meetings with Janice Chesters and then Associate Professor, Elaine Duffy, I was seconded from Aboriginal Studies in the Faculty of Arts to the School of Rural Health, mainly because I had a particular interest in the health and wellbeing of Aboriginal and Torres Strait Islander peoples; I had already written an Aboriginal health unit for the arts faculty. I was also well connected at a regional, national and international level and an active participant in Aboriginal organisations at a local level.

The School of Rural Health was a vibrant, forward-thinking school. It passionately advocated for the health and wellbeing of rural and Aboriginal people by providing leadership and support to local rural organisations, developing quality research and inspiring medical, nursing and allied health professionals to think about a career in the bush. Another unique feature of the school was its commitment to working with and building the capacity of local communities. Most of the committees within the School of Rural Health included in their management teams community representation that enhanced the work of the school and the credibility of the work they were doing. The Indigenous Health Unit had strong links to the Gippsland community and we relied on them to guide our curriculum and research initiatives. In the spirit of reciprocity we provided governance training, project leadership and committee representation.

The School of Rural Health had strong leadership in Roger Strasser and then Elaine Duffy, both of whom moved onto prestigious positions in Canada. During my time I saw eight different heads of school who were all committed to making a difference and to fighting for ongoing funding and recognition of the high quality work being performed.

The Indigenous Health Unit was established to provide leadership and develop policy across the whole of the University on Aboriginal and Torres Strait Islander health, and to encourage others to include Aboriginal and Torres Strait Islander perspectives in their programs. Some incorrectly assumed that our focus was only rural and resisted our attempts to encourage inclusion of Aboriginal health issues in their curriculum. However, those who embraced the opportunity worked closely with us to develop culturally appropriate teaching materials and helped us to deliver lectures and tutorials.

The Indigenous Health Unit had very humble beginnings with only one staff member, but its vision was to strive to be a centre of excellence in the delivery of an Aboriginal health curriculum across the University. Progress began with the employment of two new staff members, Lyell Wilson and Isabel Ellender, who had previously worked with me and were qualified to develop, deliver and assess a quality curriculum. The development of a unit, SRH2002 Aboriginal Health and Well-being, was taught both on-campus and by distance learning at the Gippsland, Peninsula and Caulfield campuses of Monash, with enrolments of 500 plus students.

Many students who wanted an Aboriginal health unit as part of their university experience were from remote, interstate or overseas areas and required special and individual attention to support their learning needs. This led to the employment of Heather Kelly who took a coordinating role with all students. Heather came with great depth of experience in the area of student support and was a valued contributor to the vision of the Indigenous Health Unit. Leanne Turnbull was employed as my personal assistant and her contribution and dedication to the unit was invaluable. As the workload increased many other staff were employed, including Anton Isaacs and Hilton Gruis. Hilton has been the director of the Indigenous Health Unit since my retirement in December 2011. Robyn Collins, Sue Barker, Ann-

Maree Nobelius and several other sessional staff, as well as the MUDRIH staff, helped with our lecture program. Janice Chesters and Mollie Burley, in particular, were dedicated to the advancement of rural and Aboriginal health and interprofessional learning, and provided a depth of knowledge and experience which they readily shared with us.

The early years

The newly developed Indigenous Health Unit provided expertise and support for the whole of Monash University and this was a challenge for the capacity of the unit. While our main focus was on medicine, nursing and health sciences, we also engaged and consulted with several other faculties, as well as local communities and key organisations such as the Victorian Aboriginal Community Controlled Health Organisation and the Victorian Aboriginal Education Unit.

As the program developed and expanded it became clear that there was a need to increase the number of academic and support staff to meet the growing needs and expectations. In Mildura, Rose Gilby was appointed as a lecturer to help develop the northern region curriculum and build partnerships with the local Aboriginal organisations and community.

Attempts to employ another person at the Bendigo Regional Clinical School were only partly successful. However, the ongoing support and encouragement of Professor Geoff Solarsh, director of the Bendigo Regional Clinical School, and Professor John Humphreys, head of research, were valued and welcomed; their expertise and passion in the area of rural health helped us overcome some of the early hurdles.

Aboriginal health curriculum

One of the first areas of inclusion of Aboriginal health was within the medical curriculum which incorporated lectures, problem-based learning scenarios and OSCEs (objective structure clinical examinations) that had Aboriginal issues embedded in them. Students were also encouraged to participate in the selective program and were offered the opportunity to attend a cultural immersion week at Iga Warta in the Flinders Ranges. Later, similar weeks were established at Mildura and Broken Hill. Twenty students per year attended these selectives over a ten year period. While they ran, they proved successful and popular in educating student doctors on Aboriginal issues and provided exemplars for similar programs in the future. The experience of the

Indigenous Health Unit is that exposing students to rural community life and allowing them to witness the challenges faced by those communities' health care needs, is far more effective than simulated exercises and lectures.

Professors Chris Browne and Ben Canny, in particular, have been great faculty supporters of the Indigenous Health Unit's work in medical student training. From within the medical student cohort the Wildfire club also supports Aboriginal health programs. Among other activities, Wildfire runs the Matthew Campbell Memorial Lecture each year to honour the memory of Matthew, one of the early advocates for Aboriginal health in the faculty. Matthew was tragically killed in a car accident before he finished his studies.

The roll-out of the Aboriginal health unit to nursing, health sciences, paramedics and sociology students was a major coup. The inclusion of the unit into these courses ensured that all graduates from our faculty would be acquainted with the issues relating to the health of Aboriginal and Torres Strait Islander people. The delivery of the unit was difficult at times as it cut across internal funding arrangements within the faculty and student reactions were variable. Nevertheless the introduction of the unit was a hugely important step in the cause of recognising the issues and improving the health of Aboriginal Australians; the Indigenous Health Unit showed the way. It was guided for many years by a strong and active Community Advisory Council which consisted of key rural and Aboriginal organisations, community leaders and members of the general public. The council provided advice on the needs of the local rural communities and provided focus on future directions for research and programs. It also enhanced the applications for funding as many of the members were strongly connected to political lobby groups and advocated for rural and Aboriginal health.

Projects

The first of the major projects undertaken by the Indigenous Health Unit was Building Healthy Communities: A Rural Chronic Disease Initiative, of which Di Wyatt was the chief investigator and program leader. Of the 26 sites the project covered, nine were Aboriginal communities. Our role was to visit and support the community initiatives, to ensure protocols were followed and that the community engaged with the project team. This was a national project that required sensitive and culturally safe approaches. The project was very successful and stimulated far greater national and international interest than had been envisaged at the beginning.

Launch of the Rural Chronic Disease Initiative 'Building Healthy Communities Resource Kit' 2004: back left to right – Keith Salvat, Marlene Drysdale; front left to right – Janice Chesters, Susan Fawkner.'

The second project – Footprints Forwards: Better Strategies for the Recruitment, Retention and Support of Indigenous Medical Students – was also a national project of which I was chief investigator and program manager. The project was undertaken by the consortium of Monash University, James Cook University and University of New South Wales, and investigated opportunities and barriers to Indigenous students' entry to medical education in Australia. It examined existing information relating to Indigenous recruitment and support, identified reasons for the low completion rates of students, reviewed existing promotional materials, developed an interactive multimedia product, designed and piloted a flexible and sustainable model of recruitment, and established a project reference group. The project's final report made eight recommendations that were intended to enhance the recruitment and retention of Indigenous medical students. The two phases of the project were completed on time and within the budget.

In collaboration with Andrology Australia, the Indigenous Health Unit was commissioned to write the Aboriginal men's health unit for Aboriginal health workers, which included culturally appropriate activities that were to focus on Aboriginal men's health needs. This project was trialled at chosen sites and is now part of a Certificate IV course for Aboriginal health workers. Hilton Gruis and Anton Isaacs both had a specific interest in Aboriginal men's mental health and were successful in obtaining a Beyond Blue research grant.

Several other staff were involved in projects while completing masters or PhD degrees. They contributed to the research capacity of the school by publishing articles in carefully targeted journals.

One of our key projects was the development and delivery of cultural safety training both for University staff and various community organisations which provided services to Aboriginal people and communities. This activity provided financial resources for the unit that allowed staff to participate in conferences and professional development activities. It also allowed for some support for community activities.

Immersion programs

One of the innovative successes of our work was the immersion programs. These programs allowed students to learn about Aboriginal culture directly from the people with lived experiences who were willing to take students on a journey of understanding through shared knowledge within an Aboriginal community. Some of the cultural activities included visits to the original Aboriginal mission sites where they heard the history from people who had lived there through hardships and happy times. Other activities included visits to sacred sites, interpretation of art sites, bush tucker and medicines as well as Aboriginal bush survival skills. These opportunities were limited to 20 medicine, 20 nursing/health science students and four staff members. The program was cultural safety in action. Students started with an understanding of the protocols required such as respect, dress code, listening, and involvement in all group activities. Each day there was a debrief session including games and a sing-along by the campfire. Students met local Aboriginal people, including elders, Traditional Owners, health workers, and traditional healers, and heard about how they work in their communities. These people were always ready to talk to students and answer any of their questions.

Awards and recognition

During the 10 years of my time at the Indigenous Health Unit we were recognised for our achievements with awards such as the Vice-Chancellor's

Excellence Award, twice; Leaders in Indigenous Medical Education Award for excellence in the recruitment and support of Aboriginal medical students; Australian GPET (General Practice Education and Training) award for registrar training; and several community awards for reconciliation, governance and community support. Other awards were given to individual staff members for their contributions to community organisations. It is important for people who work hard in their areas of expertise to be recognised for their contributions and, more importantly, acknowledged by their peers. The School of Rural Health always celebrated their achievements as a family, understanding the environment of rural and Aboriginal health and the challenges it presents.

Marlene Drysdale graduates with her Doctorate of Communication from Deakin University 2010.

Challenges

One of the challenges that the unit undertook was to increase the number of Aboriginal students in the medical courses. When the Indigenous Health Unit was established, Monash had only one Aboriginal medical student and no recruitment strategy, identified student places or support mechanisms. Within a network of other university Indigenous units and a close working relationship with the then Centre for Australian Indigenous Studies student support unit, we began a recruitment campaign to enrol more students. Our first port of call was VTAC (the Victorian Tertiary Admissions Centre) to identify Aboriginal students interested in medicine and follow them up to make sure they were prepared for the UMAT (Undergraduate Medicine and Health Sciences Admission Test). A similar approach was taken with postgraduate students to support them to sit the GAMSAT (Graduate Medical School Admissions Test) entrance exam. Our relationship with the Australian Indigenous Doctors Association resulted in some referrals. Progress required a personal approach to each student and often to their parents. We provided support for students to attend interviews and introductory sessions. After enrolment, we provided academic and personal support to enable them to complete their studies.

In 2011, 11 Aboriginal students enrolled in the medical course, proving the success of the recruitment campaign.

In 2004 the Monash University Faculty of Medicine, Nursing and Health Sciences became a signatory to the Indigenous Health Curriculum Framework developed by the Committee of Deans of Australian Medical Schools. The framework has since been included in the Australian Medical Council's accreditation guidelines for basic medical education and requires all medical schools to include core Indigenous health content in their medical curricula. The framework recognised that all medical graduates need to be both clinically and culturally competent to affect positive health outcomes for this portion of the population whose health outcomes were, and are still, unacceptably poor. The Indigenous Health Unit had the task of implementing the framework within our faculty and worked tirelessly to educate staff and students about Aboriginal health issues. The advocacy and support provided by the School of Rural Health was crucial in successfully embedding Aboriginal health as a core unit into all courses offered by the faculty. I am particularly grateful for the support of Janice Chesters, John Togno, John Humphreys and Mollie Burley at this time.

Reflections and the future

There were some wonderful and exciting times, as well as some inevitable disappointments. The commitment and tenacity of the team and our supporters always enabled us to keep moving towards achieving our goals. The Indigenous Health Unit has certainly satisfied our initial aims of providing leadership and developing policy across the whole University on Aboriginal and Torres Strait Islander health. Although there were many changes, there was always support for the work we were doing and trust in our professionalism to uphold the integrity of the school and the vision of the University.

An exciting advance in Aboriginal health has been the establishment of the School for Indigenous Health within the Faculty of Medicine, Nursing and Health Sciences at Monash. The school was built on the foundations provided by the Indigenous Health Unit, but now, with increased status and reach across the faculty, it ensures that the Aboriginal health message, education, research and support activities are able to gain maximum leverage. The school and the unit share the following aims:

- to train Aboriginal and non-Aboriginal people to more effectively address Aboriginal health
- to broker and conduct high quality research
- to support the health and community development goals of Aboriginal communities
- to provide strong governance and leadership to ensure that the whole faculty shares responsibility for Aboriginal health

Through collaboration with the School of Indigenous Health, the Unit of Indigenous Health concentrates specifically on rural aspects of the charter. It is hoped that this structure will build on the past advances made by the unit, and that it will ultimately make a significant impact on health outcomes for Aboriginal people.

Congratulations to the School of Rural Health, MUDRIH and the Indigenous Health Unit on what has been achieved in the past 20 years! On a personal note, thank you for the opportunities you have given me to follow my passion and thank you to the many wonderful people I have had the pleasure of working with. I reflect back on those times with great fondness and pride.

CHAPTER 8

ADMINISTRATION: FLYING UNDER THE RADAR

ROBERT CLOUGH

Culture

The evolution from the Monash University Centre for Rural Health in 1992 to the School of Rural Health of 2012 has been remarkable. Over the journey many staff and students have fulfilled their aspirations during their time with the school. Nevertheless, my introduction and initiation to the centre was difficult. My experience, I came to realise, was shared by countless new appointees. Initial questions of 'What does the Centre for Rural Health do?', 'What roles do people play?' and 'Where is everyone?' were soon followed by 'What am I supposed to do?' It took me 12 months to answer most of these questions!

The centre had a very loose structural framework. For those requiring firm boundaries and job descriptions that clearly provided responsibilities and expectations, the lack of direction was stressful. For those able to survive the first 12 months, a career blossomed before them enabling the best use of their skills and interests; a niche within the organisation formed around them. This has been the case for both academic and administrative staff. Although job descriptions and orientation processes provide a much smoother introduction to the school these days, a culture that allows for individual expression and growth still exists.

In the early days the centre's vision, culture and drive was provided by Professor Roger Strasser. Roger was the only person who knew everything about the centre's work – how it all fitted together and why. Many individuals represented specific blooms on the bush that was the Centre for Rural Health, but Roger not only represented the trunk and branches, he also provided the soil and the pot in which the bush grew; he had the vision and was the instigator and facilitator of every activity of the centre.

Roger had a unique personal style. He had a tremendous drive and passion for rural health that was obvious and infectious. There seemed little or no distinction between work, family or relaxation for Roger. It was nothing to be welcomed to work on Monday morning by a barrage of emails from Roger sent at 3.30 that morning, or for him, Sarah and their five children to spend the weekend at a rural health conference. Roger worked, nurtured his family and relaxed simultaneously. I'm certain that he had rural health dreams in the few hours of sleep that he did manage!

There was, however, a quirkiness to Roger. We often wondered how seriously he would be received at the faculty meetings when we farewelled him from Traralgon, dressed in his baggy unironed shorts, crinkled, opened-necked, short-sleeved shirt and roman sandals. Would his suit-wearing colleagues take him seriously as he argued the academic virtues of our centre?

Whatever the initial impression made by Roger he had a resilience that was unshakable. Whether it was a severe reprimand from the dean, a dressing down by members of the centre's executive or a funding application knock back, Roger would invariably brush himself off and redouble his efforts. Such setbacks were only momentary hiccups in the journey towards his desired outcome.

Initially the centre maintained an independence from the faculty and University primarily because the centre was 'out of sight – out of mind'. This phenomenon proved to be both a virtue and hindrance. The advantages were that we were able to sail under many procedural rules, which enabled us to set up processes and systems best suited to our circumstances. For instance, Joe Hovel, Steve Kirkbright, Dr John Togno and others set up our initial information technology network. The framework, email system, shared-drive structure and hardware were different from those at the major campuses, but were universally agreed to be the best for our requirements. Our network was envied by those in the faculty who ventured beyond the major campus limits to visit us. We were able to build up the network because we did everything. We planned, bought, installed and maintained the hardware and software ourselves. A major reason why our network functioned so well was that everything was scrutinised from a user perspective. The planners, buyers, installers and maintainers were also the users. Of course, we were able to do this because of our small size and the fact that we operated from one primary site in Gippsland.

Similar stories could be told regarding capital works projects, maintenance, human resource and finance management. We posed a difficult problem for the mainstream Monash University administration and, consequently, they were generally happy to let the minnow that was the Centre for Rural Health slip under their guard. If we were challenged later, we would plead ignorance of the rule. Monash had a vast array of policies that we could only consider if we already knew they existed!

A break between sessions in Traralgon 2003: left to right – Julie Luke, Daryl Pedler, Joanna Boast (Latrobe Regional Hospital librarian), Steve Kirkbright.

Steve Kirkbright deserves special acknowledgement. Among his many talents Steve was – and no doubt still is – a very skilled graphic designer. Every publication produced by the centre in the early years had Steve's touch on it. Whether it was an email newsletter, website, a poster being delivered by a junior academic or a presentation by Roger to government, it was universally lauded for its quality and innovative style. Steve created a 'look' for the Centre for Rural Health that was admired and envied. He had the capacity to sit for a short time with authors, then turn their jumble of data and ideas into products that conveyed the message with panache.

The down side of being 'out of sight – out of mind' was that there was very little administrative, technical or academic support, and relatively few took us seriously. If many of our new staff had trouble grasping the functions of our centre, how could we really expect those outside the organisation to know why we were there? We sought recognition on many levels for varying reasons. We needed the faculty and University to appreciate our educational and research potential before expecting their support. The communities within which we worked had to be convinced of the value of our work and its potential impact in order to sway the various levels of government towards the importance of improving rural health. We also sought recognition among local, state, national and international rural health academics for our work, in order to raise the profile of issues, and also to attract academics to our organisation. Ironically, it appeared that for some time the greater the distance people were from our centre in Gippsland, the higher our renown. We were often visited by international academics who were highly enthusiastic about our work and influence, while we were virtually unrecognised in the towns within which we operated, and by our own faculty.

Much of the effort to promote the centre involved travelling. Although we quickly became adept at using teleconferencing as a communication tool within the centre, there was little incentive for external groups to use such technology. So we would find ourselves leaving home at 5.30 am to attend an 8.00 am meeting at the metropolitan campus on a regular basis. For many years I would travel to meetings at the Clayton campus once or twice per week with at least a four-hour travel turn-around time. Not to attend the meeting would be to miss the opportunity for representation at these forums. They were opportunities to educate others, not only about our existence, but also about the exciting advances we were making. Unfortunately, time spent travelling – affecting academic and senior administrative staff – was not allowed for in work output expectations. In later years we pioneered videoconferencing as a means of attending meetings without travelling. To the faculty's credit, they ultimately recognised the value of videoconferencing, setting up a sophisticated system at faculty headquarters and encouraging its use. This has saved significant time and money, and reduced the risk of car accidents.

The evolution of the Centre for Rural Health/School of Rural Health has occurred at arm's length from the University and, although aspects of their respective visions and objectives are shared, they are not exactly the same. Monash's objectives revolve around excellence in teaching and research whereas the Centre for Rural Health/School of Rural Health vision is to improve rural health. This vision includes teaching and research, but also covers issues such as rural health workforce development and advocacy. These more applied objectives were amplified when the school received direct ongoing Rural Clinical School Project funding from the Commonwealth. The primary aim of this project is to increase the numbers of medical practitioners in rural Australia – an aim that is reinforced by funding parameters. The variation in emphasis has meant that the school has had to satisfy two requirements: the Commonwealth desire for the program to increase medical practitioners in rural areas; and Monash's demands for a teaching program that produces excellent graduates. To the school's credit, both criteria have and are being met.

Finance

Budgeting and finance within the tertiary education sector were completely foreign to me when I commenced at the Centre for Rural Health. Pathology services – which formed my professional background – worked on direct payment for service. The Centre for Rural Health/School of Rural Health funding relied on government grants and Monash/faculty funding policies. I was nervous about relying on another body's continued generosity for the maintenance of funding. I recall being aghast, on compiling an early budget with Roger, where we listed $2 million worth of expenditure but could only identify $1 million of known income. The $1 million shortfall was made up by what was, at the time, unknown 'project income'. Roger saw it as his task to attract this project funding over the proceeding months. He never failed.

I soon came to appreciate the logic of this process. The centre needed to successfully complete rural health-related education and research projects, to build a reputation that would assist us in gaining larger and more prestigious projects; we had to build a 'track record'. However, to take on these projects as they arose unpredictably throughout the year, we required access to staff with the appropriate skills and availability. Roger overcame the potential problem by employing many people across the country on very small fractions. The system appeared to me to work like this: Roger would identify people with relevant skills and a passion for rural health, and would offer them a 'retainer' fixed-term contract for a small fraction such as 0.1 or even 0.05 effective full-time. Such contracts amounted to a few hours per week. Roger kept in contact with these staff members, but quite often they did nothing for large periods of time. This would continue until Roger found funding for a project. He would piece together a project team from those available on his list and supplement them with others if required. Quite often people would work many more hours per week than their fraction, but this was offset by the months that they were being paid for being relatively idle. The value of this method was that there was an available talent pool for projects when they arose; it would have been very difficult to piece together a team at short notice otherwise.

This was all manageable while Roger was able to lead each project. The continuity of the system required some projects to subsidise others, some staff salaries to come from projects for which they did no work, and operating expenses to be borne where they could be afforded. We operated very much from hand to mouth. We had to be able to respond to opportunities when they arose and recover from shortfalls when they occurred.

Funding for the Centre for Rural Health/School of Rural Health can be categorised into five broad sources:

1. state government
2. Commonwealth Government via Monash University
3. Commonwealth Government direct
4. research
5. other project funding.

The relative proportions from these funding sources have varied greatly over time and in many ways reflect the evolution of the School of Rural Health.

When the Centre for Rural Health was founded its only role was to provide rural placement sites for medical students. As such, its only source of income was Commonwealth funding, provided via Monash University and the faculty. As the centre became established it became involved in many different projects and programs such as vocational training for general practitioners (Victorian Advanced Training for General Practitioners); health career and course information for secondary school students (the Secondary Schools Project); and small local projects such as the Moe After Hours Medical Service. Another phase was reached when rural clinical school funding was received directly from the Commonwealth. This included initial funding for capital works and was followed by ongoing funding for the operating costs of providing clinical medical education in rural locations. Following the establishment of the rural clinical schools, including Monash's four regional clinical schools, major funding grants have been attracted for the Northern Victoria Regional Medical Education Network – in collaboration with the University of Melbourne – Monash

University Department of Rural and Indigenous Health, and the Centre of Research Excellence in Rural and Remote Primary Health Care. All these developments have changed the balance of what we have been paid to do. However, the body of water that is the school has swollen to the point where the addition of new programs now merely creates small waves where tsunamis could have resulted previously.

The growth in the quantum of the School of Rural Health expenditure budget over my years as manager is evidence of the huge expansion of the organisation in that time. Our expenditure budget in 2000 was around $2 million but rose to over $30 million when establishing the regional clinical school sites. With the recent, welcome inclusion of the Gippsland Medical School under the School of Rural Health umbrella, the budget has continued to expand.

Capital works

In 2001 it was announced that Monash's application for funding to establish a rural clinical school had been successful. Our ambitious plan was to develop regional clinical schools in Mildura, Bendigo and East Gippsland, an office of head of school in Moe, and a rural office on the main metropolitan campus at Clayton. Existing facilities in Traralgon would become a fourth regional clinical school site. State and federal governments initially pledged $4.5 million each – $9 million in total over three years for capital works. This exciting news posed a logistical dilemma: we faced running 13 separate projects across Victoria as well as developing 12 new general practice training locations. Mildura and East Gippsland had to be developed from scratch. Although we had some staff in Bendigo, this site also had to be developed from the ground up. Each site was different with opportunities and circumstances unique to its location.

We applied a few general philosophies as we sought solutions. It was important to forge relationships with health services within the regions, to ensure the ongoing viability of our programs, and to be mindful of our vision to improve rural health. The facilities that we built should provide benefit for the heath service and local community as well as for our students and staff. (What regional health service does not need access to large meeting spaces with state-of-the-art audio visual equipment?) As well as using the capital works to help nurture trusting relationships with the health services, it was important to provide students with comfortable accommodation while on their rural placements.

1998. The new facilities at Latrobe Regional Hospital, Traralgon, popularly referred to as 'Roger's ring'.

One director of medical services at a regional health service had formed the following opinion of universities following his time at a metropolitan health service: 'I regard universities as a boil on the backside of any health service where their students are placed!' He explained that, in his experience, the universities absorbed all that the health service could give them, but then still took more. We set out to change this mindset, at least in regard to the regional sites from which we operated.

We went to the health services with the following proposal: we wished to establish facilities within their organisation to enable our students to pursue their clinical training. The facilities could be tutorial rooms, a library, office and administrative areas and somewhere for the students to relax. The facilities could be used by the health service. Once the works were completed they would be handed over to the health service to be leased back at a peppercorn rental for a period calculated on the quantity of project funds spent on the capital works.

In some cases there were greenfield sites available on the health service campus; in others existing buildings were renovated, and in some instances land was purchased. The 13 initial capital works projects were:

1. renovation of a previous ward at the now closed Latrobe Valley Hospital in Moe for an office of head of school
2. renovation of the former nurses' home at Latrobe Valley Hospital for student accommodation
3. construction of new student accommodation on the West Gippsland Healthcare Group hospital campus in Warragul
4. construction of new clinical school facilities and student accommodation at Mildura Base Hospital
5. purchase of Lister House in Bendigo (former Central Victorian School of Nursing, then Department of Health regional office) for research and administration offices as well as student accommodation
6. renovation of Lister House student accommodation
7. purchase of properties in Mercy Street, Bendigo, to build clinical teaching facilities and library
8. construction of clinical teaching facilities and a library in Mercy Street, Bendigo
9. construction of a primary care clinic in Bendigo
10. renovations at Monash University's Clayton campus to create a rural health office and facilities for the students' rural club, Wildfire
11. renovation of existing buildings at Central Gippsland Hospital in Sale for teaching spaces, library, offices and student accommodation
12. construction of new clinical school buildings on the Bairnsdale Regional Health hospital campus
13. construction of student accommodation in Day Street, Bairnsdale.

The school engaged a project officer, Greg Beevor, and a project planning consultant, Raf Dua, to help coordinate these projects and to deal directly with architects and builders. We established project control groups for each project, which included representatives of the health services that were directly impacted. As well as coordinating the projects, we had to provide the regular reports required by the funding bodies. Those were certainly busy and exciting times.

We briefed the Monash University Facility and Services Division on our intentions and plans at a very early stage. After receiving guarantees that they would not become encumbered with responsibilities for building cleaning and maintenance they were happy for us to proceed. The division offered to provide a project manager to attend project control group meetings but his attendance discontinued after a short time due to his other commitments; the division was extremely busy with other major projects within the university. It appeared that we were 'flying under the radar' once more.

We embarked on the projects with energetic zeal, ignorant of the myriad policies and regulations that surround Monash University capital works projects. We became aware of procedures sometime after the projects were completed, when the Facilities and Services Division finally caught up with us! Despite this, all the projects were delivered on time and within budget.

Since the initial flurry of capital works, the school has been involved in a number of subsequent projects such as major extensions to the East Gippsland Regional Clinical School, Bendigo Regional Clinical School and Mildura Regional Clinical School. The number of teaching general practices that have benefited from supported capital works has increased from 12 to around 25.

The capital works projects enabled the development of productive, trusting relationships with the health services in the regions in which we operated. We were able to prove that we could deliver on our promises, add value to health services and be trusted not to take advantage of them. We certainly were not 'a boil on their backside'!

People and relationships

Relationship building has been integral in the evolution of the Centre for Rural Health/School of Rural Health. This has been particularly the case for administrative and professional staff. Relationships have been crucial with local communities and health services, with faculty administrators and with Monash University central services. Maintenance of these relationships has required special effort particularly when distance and remoteness are taken into account. Empathy is required when explaining to local non-university people why certain administrative functions cannot happen instantly, because of the constraints imposed by University policies and procedures. Trips to Clayton were often required to meet personally with faculty and central university staff to discuss unique issues affecting the rural programs. It is too easy to be brushed aside when communicating by telephone to someone buried within a huge bureaucratic maze.

The administrative roles and expectations were different at the School of Rural Health. Administrative positions were decision-making roles imbued with responsibility: quite often the buck stopped with people in these positions because there was no-one else to pass the buck to! We have been asked many times to explain why we had such a high administration to academic staff ratio and to justify administrative positions. The reasons were the high number of fractional-time clinical teachers employed at our regional clinical schools, and our multi-site structure. Due to their high clinical load, teaching clinicians merely arrived at scheduled times to take tutorials, then left. They performed no administrative duties, not even timesheet completion. Even our regional directors were part-time, with full-time clinical roles on top of their Monash University responsibilities. The regional administrators were also responsible for student accommodation and often, by extension, student welfare. And finally, a structure of multiple small sites required much more administration than a few major sites. A gunshot fired through any of our regional sites in the early days would have had little chance of striking an academic! The result was that the rural administrators were responsible for running the operation and played key roles in planning the future.

Along with playing critical roles regionally, administrators also played a crucial cross-school role. A management group was formed that included the key administrators. This group met, and still meets, monthly via videoconference and twice a year, face-to-face. The matters considered by the group include financial and budgetary issues, internal and University human resource policies and procedures, student accommodation and welfare, teaching and learning administrative issues and research administration. The group has provided a reliable communication route for horizontal information transfer throughout the school and is a mechanism for bi-directional vertical interaction with the School of Rural Health executive committee. The management group has been able to share knowledge and expertise in dealing with issues as they have arisen, and has produced policies and procedures that have ensured consistency. In 2008 the School of Rural Health management group received the Vice-Chancellor's Award for Exceptional Performance by Professional Staff. The group consisted of Graham Allardice, Vicki Dane, Elaine Evans, Jenny Donelly, Michael Elswyk, Marg Bibic, Lisa Lavey, Louise Bassam, Laura Salamone (now Major) and Carolyn Vaughan. This group, individually and collectively, had a massive influence on the successful establishment of the Monash University regional clinical school sites and programs across Victoria.

Another professional staff member to receive recognition via a Vice-Chancellor's Award for Excellence was long-serving Gippsland stalwart, Julie Luke. Julie started work at the Centre for Rural Health as a shy administrative assistant who blossomed into a key clinical year coordinator, much loved by staff and students alike.

Vice-Chancellor's award for exceptional performance by professional staff 2008: back row left to right – Laura Major, Elaine Evans, Jenny Donelly, Graham Allardice, Lisa Lavey, Marg Bibic; front row left to right – Carolyn Vaughan, Robert Clough, Louise Bassam, Michael Elswyk.

Julie's colleague in Gippsland, Elaine Evans, is our longest-serving employee. Elaine began work as an administrative assistant with Roger in a small room in Moe, infamously described as a 'broom closet', in the very early days of the organisation. Subsequently she has worked as Roger's personal assistant, as the human resources manager and is currently manager of the Gippsland Regional Clinical School. Along with her expertise and knowledge of the organisation's history, Elaine's bubbly nature and good humour have made her a very popular staff member.

Graham Allardice is the current senior operations manager of the School of Rural Health. In the ten years that he has been with the school, Graham has managed the development of the Bendigo Regional Clinical School's evolution from an office of four staff to a multi-million dollar state-of-the-art clinical school building which accommodates over 45 staff. Graham has managed the complexities of such incredible growth with considerable skill, blended with his unique empathy for those around him. In 2006 Graham's work was formally recognised when he received the Dean's Award for Excellence in Administration.

Others who deserve individual acknowledgement are Vicki Dane, Mildura Regional Clinical School, and Jenny Donelly, East Gippsland Regional Clinical School. Vicki and Jenny have overcome the problems associated with establishing regional clinical schools in the most remote corners of Victoria. They have done so with a mixture of skill, patience, devotion and a large dose of determination! The two regional clinical schools have developed into jewels in the Centre for Rural Health/School of Rural Health crown that provides students with idiosyncratic, quality, medical training.

Meeting in Melbourne at a strategic planning exercise 2004: left to right – Cheryl Sutherland, Vicki Dane, Megan McNair.

There have been many more professional staff who have provided dedicated and devoted service over the years. The combined contributions made by professional staff have built and maintained the foundations upon which a highly regarded academic institution has flourished.

Leadership

I have had the pleasure of working with a number of heads of school, each of whom has added a unique and valuable character and emphasis to the organisation. I have written of Roger and his vision and passion previously. Roger's positive influence is still felt within the organisation he founded as well as nationally and internationally. Following Roger's departure for Canada the school was in a state of flux for the best part of two years as a successor was sought. During that time several senior staff members attempted to 'keep the balls in the air', taking on the role of acting head of school while continuing to perform their substantive roles. These were Associate Professor (now Professor) Elaine Duffy, Professor John Humphreys, Professor Gordon Whyte, and lastly the dean, Professor Nick Saunders. In truth it was a difficult time. Finally Professor Geoff Solarsh was recruited from South Africa. What Geoff lacked in local knowledge was made up for by his strategic approach and attention to detail. Geoff took the school from a band of dedicated and effective amateurs to a group of academic units, depending less on enthusiasm and more on best practice academic methods. His support for research positions resulted in the recruitment of some excellent researchers and increased research output. Geoff's meticulous attention to budgetary issues was instrumental in negotiating some difficult financial times. With Geoff's decision to concentrate on the leadership of the Northern Victoria Regional Medical Education Network, Professor Gordon Whyte took over the role of head of school. Gordon had the task of recruiting a new head of school while providing leadership in times when the north-western regional clinical schools were heading in one direction (via the Northern Victoria Regional Medical Education Network) and the south-eastern regional clinical schools were heading in another (via the Gippsland Medical School); the research unit and Monash University Department of Rural and Indigenous Health were caught somewhere in between. Gordon did well with both areas, resulting in the excellent appointment of Professor Judi Walker as head of school and passing over to her a healthy and vibrant institution.

We have been led by an active and diverse executive committee which has reflected the school's diverse interests including medical education, research, multidiscipline health, workforce, Aboriginal health, gender and administration. It can be difficult to operate a democratic model within a largely authoritarian structure such as a university; however, this committee has managed to do so. Many of the meetings have featured fiercely fought debates, but all have been respectful and sincere in the objective of honouring our vision: to improve rural health.

It has been a privilege to work for the Monash University School of Rural Health and a delight to be involved in the evolution of what has become an outstanding organisation.

Current head of school, Judi Walker, 2011. Photo: Monash University Gippsland

CHAPTER 9

GIPPSLAND MEDICAL SCHOOL: TAKING ADVANTAGE OF OPPORTUNITIES AS THEY ARISE

ASSOCIATE PROFESSOR WILLIAM HART, PROFESSOR JUDI WALKER, ASSOCIATE PROFESSOR SHANE BULLOCK

The first graduates from the Gippsland Medical School of Monash University started as interns in 2012. As a result of their experience of being trained in Gippsland, many will choose to return to rural areas to provide services to otherwise underserviced populations. To date, for 2013, all 10 Gippsland Regional Intern Training places have been accepted by Gippsland Medical School graduates.

In 2006, funding was approved for Monash to establish extra Commonwealth Supported Places in the medical program. This funding involved the establishment of a new graduate entry program at Monash's Churchill campus in Gippsland – the Gippsland Medical School – and the Extended Rural Cohort of students to undertake most of their three-year clinical placements in north-western Victoria. In this graduate entry version of the Monash medical degree, students achieve their degree in four years, rather than the five required by direct entry – school-leaver – students at Clayton and in Malaysia.

Capital grants from state and federal governments totalling $12 million enabled infrastructure upgrades at the Churchill campus to create the medical school base, and also at the clinical sites of the new school. These included those affiliated with the School of Rural Health's two regional clinical schools in Gippsland and at Peninsula Health at Frankston, a major outer south-eastern metropolitan hospital bordering the Gippsland region.

Extra Commonwealth Supported Places were sourced in 2007 and 2008. Gippsland Medical School took its first intake of 57 students in

2008, growing to 89 in 2012. The 2012 student number consisted of 65 Commonwealth Supported Places with the balance made up of international students.

Gippsland Medical School achieved full accreditation from the Australian Medical Council at the first attempt. There have been no problems attracting a good quality student cohort, including local and international students, both Commonwealth Supported and full fee paying.

On 1 January 2011 the Gippsland Medical School was amalgamated with the School of Rural Health. As originally conceived and established, Gippsland Medical School was in an ambivalent position in relation to the regional clinical schools in Gippsland. This move relieved the tensions generated by different approaches to rural medical education and competition for clinical places in Gippsland, paving the way for the next era in the School of Rural Health's growth and development.

Foundations

Staff

The Gippsland Medical School founding head was Professor Chris Browne, who worked with the Pro Vice-Chancellor of the Churchill campus – Professor Brian McKenzie and then Dr Harry Ballis – to lay the human and physical foundations for the new medical school.

Chris, a thirty-year Monash veteran, had first come to the Department of Biochemistry in the medical faculty at Monash from Oxford, UK, before heading off to become a research fellow in medicine at McGill University in Montreal. He rejoined Monash in the Department of Physiology in January 1982. He spent 10 years as part of the fetal physiology research program led by Professor Geoff Thorburn. From 1995 he took on many leadership roles within the faculty, developing and designing medical courses and programs. In 1999, he helped develop and introduce the faculty's new school structure with the dean, Professor Nick Saunders.

In 2002 Chris was elected as the first president of the Monash University academic board. During 2004–2005 he established the College of Medicine at the University of Sharjah in the United Arab Emirates and also played a lead role in the establishment of the Monash Medical School in Malaysia. He established Gippsland Medical School in July 2006 and then in 2010 he took up a position in the office of the Vice-Chancellor working to establish the Southeast University-Monash University Joint

Graduate School and Research Institute in China, a position from which he retired in July 2012.

Associate Professor William Hart was recruited by Chris in November 2006 as deputy head to lead the managerial aspects of establishing the new medical school. With a background as a public health physician, William was also involved in establishing various aspects of the Year A curriculum, particularly in the areas of personal and professional development, population health, and problem-based learning. William became head of school in 2010 and then director in 2011 under the new School of Rural Health organisational structure, prior to being recruited by Curtin University in Perth in September 2012 as foundation head and professor of medicine.

The vital task of conversion and contextualisation of the Monash medical curriculum from a five-year course into a four-year rural and outer metropolitan program fell to Associate Professor Robyn Hill, who had worked with Chris previously on the new Monash five-year curriculum and also had experience in the School of Rural Health. Robyn was appointed as Gippsland Medical School director of curriculum. In 2010 she left the medical school and later took up a senior management position at Central Gippsland TAFE.

These three foundation staff recruited a team of professional and academic staff to enable admission of the first cohort of students in 2008.

The directors of the Gippsland-based regional clinical schools of the School of Rural Health – Associate Professors David Campbell and Daryl Pedler were both closely involved in the establishment of Gippsland Medical School and were integral to the executive team. Both made major contributions to the development of the clinical curriculum.

With William Hart's departure in September 2012, Associate Professor Shane Bullock has been appointed acting director of the medical school to lead and manage the graduate entry medical program as the School of Rural Health moves into its next phase.

Students

No particular prerequisite undergraduate studies are required for application to the graduate entry medical program at Gippsland Medical School. Students have varied academic backgrounds and life experiences – from pharmacy to journalism, arts-law to aerospace engineering. This poses unique pedagogical challenges and opportunities. In the same class might be a student with no background in human biology and a PhD graduate in neuroscience. They learn from each other. For teaching staff, finding the optimal level of depth and breadth of material as well as a balance between didactic and self-directed learning, is an ongoing task. Exit evaluation interviews and feedback from employers indicate that the quality of graduates is high, particularly in the area of clinical skills, irrespective of undergraduate background.

Predictors of return to working in a rural region include the student coming from a rural area, as well as exposure to rural medicine during the course. Gippsland Medical School has strategies to recruit students of rural origin at rates in excess of the Commonwealth's medical student target of 25 per cent and to ensure that the list of applicants has a sufficient number of potential students of rural and Gippsland origin.

There are major challenges in attracting students who were born and bred in the bush. Gippsland Medical School engages with local secondary schools to improve their students' health literacy and to raise expectations that rural and Indigenous students can apply to enter the Monash medical degree. With Gippsland Medical School part of the School of Rural Health, a whole-of-school approach is being taken to increase rural admissions into the medical degree across both direct and graduate entry student cohorts.

Managing a dispersed rural cohort model

As one of four cohorts of medical students managed by Monash, the challenge for Gippsland Medical School was to contextualise and deliver the Monash medical degree appropriately with respect to the issues of rural and Indigenous health in Gippsland, while achieving equivalent academic outcomes as Monash medical students from Clayton, Malaysia or the Extended Rural Cohort. In the rural cohorts, this challenge is compounded by the community-based teaching model of student attachments to small rural hospitals and general practice clinics, which requires close coordination and academic support. Through a regionalised committee structure and a commitment to communication, staff in the network of hospitals, community centres and private medical clinics collaborate with Monash staff to maintain the integrity of the course.

Monash's is a generalist medical degree and the learning outcomes achieved are equivalent whether the student is trained in Gippsland, Clayton or Malaysia. In the regional clinical schools in Gippsland a model of training has been developed which contextualises the curriculum around problems and cases which illustrate rural and Indigenous issues.

The first cohort of Gippsland Medical School students graduated in December 2011.

The first year, Year A, of the curriculum at Gippsland Medical School, is unique. In contrast to the direct entry course offered at Clayton and Malaysia, the graduate entry cohort is significantly smaller and students have a one-year foundation program instead of two. The current Year A program is a mix of problem-based, other small group learning modes, seminar/workshops and didactic teaching. In a one-year program there are some great opportunities for alignment and integration of the curriculum themes and assessment. Much of the learning is contextualised to demonstrate rural and/or Indigenous issues. The social, population health and biomedical components of the program focus on the relevance to clinical practice. Within weeks of commencing Year A, the students participate in significant out-placement in clinics and hospitals. In addition, all students undertake extended placements with community service and support agencies. The feedback from students is that Year A is intensive and challenging for many of them. They value highly clinical skills learning, the rapport they develop with Gippsland Medical School staff and the anatomy program.

The funding for the new medical student places was designed to overcome the medical workforce shortage in Gippsland and, as a consequence, the medical school has high expectations placed upon it by the local community. The very nature of the rural community and its relative closeness to the Gippsland campus necessitates a closer relationship than in the more anonymous metropolitan environment. Gippsland Medical School and the two Gippsland regional clinical schools have retained a high level of public and local political interest since their establishment. Recent developments within Monash aiming to increase the autonomy of the Gippsland campus, including the Gippsland Medical School, will need to be managed very sensitively. The perceived relative merits of its graduates is an important issue for the medical school and its community partners.

Amalgamation with the School of Rural Health

As originally conceived and established, Gippsland Medical School was in a conflicting position in relation to the School of Rural Health's regional clinical schools in Gippsland. On top of this, an expansive approach to acquisition of staff and other resources led to a financial crisis within four years. This was at a time when Monash was introducing a series of measures aimed at improving its overall cost-effectiveness. In that context, it could not accumulate further debt and ways had to be found for Gippsland Medical School to operate within its means.

The tensions between Gippsland Medical School and the School of Rural Health were further fuelled by differences in approaches to rural medical education and the fact that the regional clinical schools were well funded through the Commonwealth's Rural Clinical Schools Program. In Gippsland there was increasing competition for clinical places as the regional clinical schools had responsibilities to support Clayton-based direct entry students as well as graduate entry Gippsland Medical School students.

In 2010 an opportunity for a new organisational structure arose when Chris Browne was recruited to lead the Monash China project and a new head – Professor Judi Walker – was recruited to lead the School of Rural Health.

The immediate issue was to define the relationship between the School of Rural Health and Gippsland Medical School. The Gippsland and East Gippsland Regional Clinical Schools, Gippsland Medical School, MUDRIH, the deputy dean MBBS, and the Pro Vice-Chancellor Monash Gippsland broadly agreed that it would benefit the medical program, the future of Gippsland's rural medical workforce and the Monash Gippsland campus for the Gippsland Medical School to amalgamate with the School of Rural Health.

The agreed goal was to embed, over a five-year period, a consistent, high quality rural medical education and research program for Gippsland that is carefully aligned with the Extended Rural Cohort program in the north-west and the wider Monash medical degree and draws on the education and research capacity of MUDRIH and the School of Rural Health's research office.

Different approaches to the delivery of the rural medical degree by the East Gippsland and the Gippsland Regional Clinical Schools and Gippsland Medical School are seen as strengths and are based on the principle of responsiveness to the local environment.

The underpinning tenets of the amalgamation included:

- agreement on the most appropriate model – to complement the Extended Rural Cohort and the central medical degree models – for Gippsland rural medical education with responsibility, incentives and support for both Clayton-based and Gippsland Medical School medical students
- the heads of the entities that make up the School of Rural Health to be titled 'directors' and report directly to the head of school

- the Gippsland Medical School deficit to be cleared by the faculty prior to amalgamation
- adoption of a financial model to deliver a sustainable medical program in Gippsland
- academic and professional staff positions, roles and responsibilities in the south-east region to be reviewed to identify synergies and efficiencies in the context of the School of Rural Health as a whole
- a Gippsland rural medical education identity to be defined based on the principle of enhanced workforce outcomes spanning student selection policy as a pathway for recruitment of Gippsland-origin students, curriculum interpretation and course delivery
- agreement on appropriate learning objectives and resources to support a distributed model of rural medical education
- synergistic and collaborative research initiatives across the entities that make up the School of Rural Health
- partnership and collaborative initiatives and appointments with Gippsland hospital and health services and clinical training networks at all levels
- engagement with local communities of interest to support rural medical and health professional training and research.

An amalgamation transition team led by Judi Walker was established to oversee the transition, taking responsibility for both business and academic issues. In June 2011 the amalgamation transition team undertook a six-month review of progress against the broad thematic headings that had guided its activities. They found that the task of managing the transition had been achieved, but a different structure was required to manage longer term developments.

An important goal for the School of Rural Health is to respond to the need for a sustainable medical workforce in Gippsland by developing a high quality rural medical education program that is carefully articulated and aligned with the school's Extended Rural Cohort program and the wider Monash medical degree. This was named the Gippsland Health Education Program and is managed by the Gippsland health education group.

The Gippsland health education group reports to the head of school and the School of Rural Health executive and is responsible for developing strategies to meet priorities, define and realise benefits, and monitor risks, quality and timeliness.

One of the first innovations under this new structure was for students in the graduate entry stream to have enhanced access to metropolitan clinical placements and for students in the direct entry stream to have access to Gippsland clinical placements. Under this arrangement, the distinction between 'graduate entry student' and 'undergraduate student' is blurred, after pre-clinical training, into an integrated whole-of-Monash medical cohort.

Towards a regional approach to medical education and training

By the end of 2011 the Gippsland health education group had developed a rural medical education component of the Gippsland health professions education and training model that was:

- responsive to rural medical workforce needs
- regionally specific, flexible and simple
- easily marketed and understood by prospective students, supervisors and stakeholders
- focused on training in teams and interprofessional learning.

The Gippsland health professions education and training model traverses the continuum of medical training. It is concerned with delivering the medical curriculum across the Gippsland region through contextualised learning objectives that are responsive to the region's population health needs, and demonstrating consistency in student recruitment, support and assessment across the region. It incorporates the values of innovation, social accountability, collaboration, community engagement, inclusiveness and respect. Above all it aligns with the school's Northern Victoria Regional Medical Education Network/Extended Rural Cohort program.

This model and its functions were endorsed by the School of Rural Health's executive at the end of 2011. The business case for a two-year project to implement an appropriate and sustainable structure to support the model was endorsed by the dean, Professor Christina Mitchell, in July 2012.

The School of Rural Health is now embarking on an ambitious project to achieve a regionalised medical education model for Gippsland – the next step in its continuing evolution.

AFTERWORD: LEARNING FROM THE PAST FOR A SUSTAINABLE FUTURE

PROFESSOR JUDI WALKER

It has been an exciting and humbling experience to read about the evolution of the Monash University School of Rural Health over the past 20 years. It has reinforced for me the responsibility I carry in leading the school into its third decade. There is much to be learnt from the past for future sustainability.

The preface of this book provides an excellent summary of the story of the school from the perspective of a number of people, internal and external, who have played significant roles. From a small rural academic unit in Gippsland to one of the largest and most geographically dispersed schools in the Faculty of Medicine, Nursing and Health Science at Monash University, the School of Rural Health now has a footprint that extends across Victoria from Mildura in the west to Orbost in the east. While the school is represented as two distinct regions, the Office of the Head of School provides leadership and direction across these regions. The north-west constituency consists of the Bendigo and Mildura Regional Clinical Schools and the south-east includes the Gippsland and East Gippsland Regional Clinical Schools, the Gippsland Medical School and the Monash University Department of Rural and Indigenous Health. The Office of the Head of School houses a secretariat, rural health education programs and the research hub.

The Monash academic governance structure does not accommodate small schools (size determined by sustainable teaching and research income and outputs). For the School of Rural Health to be constant to its vision of better health outcomes for rural and regional communities through high quality education, training and research programs, it needs to act as a school with one voice to thrive in the Monash family. We are seeing, in other universities, unsustainable rural health units, including rural clinical schools and university departments of rural health, incorporated into larger schools of public health and health sciences. The Monash School of Rural Health is uniquely placed as the exemplar of academic rural health, nationally and internationally. It has a unique geographical distribution of regional clinical schools and the graduate entry medical program that are each responsive to their communities, delivering distinctive and innovative models of rural medical training; a university department of rural health that is carving a defined niche as an academic leader in rural mental health, population health and interprofessional programs; and a research hub with a centre of research excellence and a growing reputation for research training in rural health. The potential is limitless for these component parts of the school to sustain and thrive by drawing on and sharing experiences and expertise in, for example, simulated learning environments, or cultural safety. There is however a danger to guard against: that continuing fragmentation, internal competition and historical feuding might turn this strength to weakness.

The school's first 10 years (1992–2001) stands as a pioneering era which saw development of a wide range of specific rural health education, workforce, research and community initiatives as well as multidisciplinary education for rural health practitioners. These provided the prototype for Australian initiatives which now fall under the banner of the Commonwealth Government's Rural Clinical Training and Support and University Department of Rural Health funded programs. It saw extension to north-west Victoria and in 2001 the establishment of the Bendigo and Mildura Regional Clinical Schools and, in the south-east, the Gippsland and East Gippsland Regional Clinical Schools. The decade culminated in the formal creation of the School of Rural Health as a fully fledged school within the Faculty of Medicine, Nursing and Health Science.

The next five years (2002–2006) generated further expansion, growth and opportunistic endeavours with the dominance of and considerable increase in medical undergraduate clinical training through the regional clinical schools. Necessary to these successes were significant degrees of engagement with health services and communities and innovations in training models. In 2006, the Gippsland Medical School (graduate entry medical program, not within the School of Rural Health) and the Extended Rural Cohort program in the north-west were established. And finally, the Centre for Multi-Disciplinary Studies in Rural Health received University Department of Rural Health funding and became Monash University Department of Rural and Indigenous Health. One nagging issue has been addressed through the contribution to this book of the then Commonwealth Minister for Health. The reason why Monash was not successful in the first and competitive University Department of Rural Health funding round in 1997 was because 'the consensus within my department was that the University of Melbourne bid for Shepparton was a better proposition' and not because Monash already had the Centre for Rural Health, a belief widely held within the school.

An outsider looking in could be forgiven for thinking that by 2006 the school's centre of gravity had shifted to the north-west at the expense of the south-east and that the employment of medical specialists was eroding the focus on primary care and a strong multidisciplinary culture. However, this shift reflects the remarkable evolution of the school. Its leaders had the ability to respond to openings afforded by the political environment to bid for new Commonwealth Supported Places for medical students and finance for capital infrastructure to support these places in rural and regional Victoria. The strength of the School of Rural Health was in seizing these opportunities as they arose and this is continuing today through the auspices of Health Workforce Australia. It will continue into the future as new trends emerge, such as the current move towards vertical integration in medical and health professions training.

The period 2007–2010 was an era of consolidation, with individual sites and regions building on successes and innovations by implementing distinctive training models, embedding rural health into the medical programs, and inroads into and breakthroughs in improving the health of Indigenous communities. The student voice was significant as students are the best advocates to promote rural clinical training.

Through the rigorous and systematic approach of the school's Office of Research, Monash has played a significant role in generating new knowledge relating to overcoming rural health workforce shortages, developing innovative rural models of health care, and understanding the risk determinants that underpin rural health disadvantage. Monash is an international leader in rural health research. The strategic approach to research that was adopted has had a significant impact on the development of new knowledge as well as on national policies. The Monash University research strategy imperatives of excellence, relevance and impact provide the necessary framework for the future.

The current era (2011 and beyond) is seeing a process of renewal through a period of change and uncertainty. It should be remembered as a period when the school achieved full academic recognition through high quality, excellence and innovation; a period which embraced a whole-of-systems approach, through partnerships and collaborations, to harness precious resources in a shrinking financial environment.

On 1 January 2011 the Gippsland Medical School was amalgamated with the School of Rural Health. As originally conceived and established, Gippsland Medical School was in a conflicting position in relation to the regional clinical schools in Gippsland. Amalgamation relieved the tensions generated by different approaches to rural medical education and competition for clinical places in Gippsland, paving the way for the next era in the School of Rural Health's development.

The current academic environment is highly competitive and the emphasis on strong national and international collaborations will require the School of Rural Health to continue to broaden its outlook and processes of engagement. In order to remain a leader in academic rural health, the school will need to build on the factors that have led to its present success. It will also be compelled to address new challenges including building stronger relationships across all units that constitute the school and responding speedily to the requirements of Monash, governments, policy makers and partner organisations.

Inevitably the initial rural health education and research pioneers are moving on. The focus must be on attracting and retaining the next generation of academic and clinical leaders who have passion and commitment to rural and regional practice and who recognise that embedding and integrating rural health training and research is integral to both the daily as well as the strategic culture of universities, health services and communities.

As a fully fledged member of the Monash family, the School of Rural Health is required to meet University requirements and expectations of its teaching and research and to succeed we must have staff adequately prepared to meet these expectations. The School of Rural Health must be indispensable to Monash medical and health professions training.

The next decade will be about balance and sustainability with a strong program of education, training, research and engagement across the school. We will see digital technologies harnessed for rural health care, education training and research and the expansion of non-traditional clinical training environments. We will see rural and regional medical and health professional training at the forefront of new models and trends, such as graduate training programs that are integrated across the training continuum. It will be imperative for the Monash School of Rural Health to keep ahead of the game in order to maintain currency and to respond to inevitable challenges, changes and opportunities.

Over 20 years the School of Rural Health has come full circle. The difference is that it is now operating as a fully fledged and recognised academic school within the largest faculty of Australia's largest university. However, we must never lose sight of the main aim – better health outcomes for rural and regional communities through leadership in and integration of responsive, sustainable and high quality education, training and research programs.

The fact that we are celebrating the twentieth anniversary of the School of Rural Health is due to thousands of people we are not able to name – health professionals, patients, community members, students, faculty, professional colleagues, bureaucrats and politicians – in addition to the many people named in the pages of this commemorative publication. Thank you. We will do everything we can to chart a pathway into the future to continue, strengthen and sustain the academic rural health journey.